ARTEFACTOS

Colombian Crafts
from the Andes to the Amazon

RIZZOLI
NEW YORK

LILIANA VILLEGAS
BENJAMIN VILLEGAS

ARTEFACTOS

Colombian Crafts from the Andes to the Amazon

RIZZOLI
NEW YORK

First published in the United States of America in 1992 by
RIZZOLI INTERNATIONAL PUBLICATIONS, INC.
300 Park Avenue South, New York, NY 10010

Copyright © 1992 by
VILLEGAS EDITORES
Carrera 13 No. 33-74. Office 303.
P. O. BOX: 7427, Bogotá, Colombia.

Library of Congress Cataloging-in-Publication Data:
Villegas, Benjamín.
Artefactos: Colombian crafts from the Andes to the Amazon
Benjamín and Liliana Villegas.
Includes bibliographical references.
ISBN 0-8478-1503-X
1. Folk art—Colombia. 2. Decorative arts—Colombia
I. Villegas, Liliana. II Title.
NK904. V55 1992   91-37255
745'.09861—dc20   CIP

Printed and bound in Japan by Toppan Printing Co., Ltd.

Directed, Designed, and Edited by
BENJAMIN VILLEGAS, LILIANA VILLEGAS

Photography: JOSE FERNANDO MACHADO,
JORGE EDUARDO ARANGO, DIEGO SAMPER,
DIEGO MIGUEL GARCES, and others
Texts: ENRIQUE PULECIO
Historic research and Glossary: GUILLERMO VERA
Graphic and editing coordinator: PILAR GOMEZ
Art coordinator: MERCEDES CEDEÑO

CAPTIONS FOR INITIAL PAGES.
FRONT JACKET: *Traditional* vueltiao *hats made from
plant fiber. San Andrés de Sotavento, Córdoba.*
BACK JACKET. *Cotton* chinchorros—*or hammocks—from Guajira.*
ENDPAPERS. *A finely stitched* mola *cloth of the Cuna Indians. Golfo de Urabá.*
PAGE 1. *A wooden panel used by shamans in healing ceremonies. Amazonas.*
PAGES 2–3. *Plant fiber basketry. Vaupés.*
PAGE 5. *A golden funerary mask. A.D. XI century. Calima culture.*
PAGE 8. *Detail of pre-Columbian funerary urn. XI century B.C. Tamalameque, Cesar.*
PAGE 9. *A pre-Columbian mask made from a seashell.
III century B.C.–A.D. II century. Tumaco culture.*
PAGE 12. *A clay jar. A.D. X century. Quimbaya culture.*
PAGE 15. *Spectators at the* corraleja—*a popular version of the Spanish
bullfight—etched into this contemporary calabash bowl. Sampués, Sucre.*
PAGE 17. *A papier-mâché carnival mask. L. Dafanor, Santafé de Antioquia.*
PAGE 19. *A brightly painted country bus. Rionegro, Antioquia.*
PAGES 20–21. *The cotton poncho and straw hat are part of the traditional
dress of the coffee-growing region. Aguadas, Caldas.*

CONTENTS

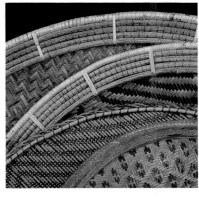

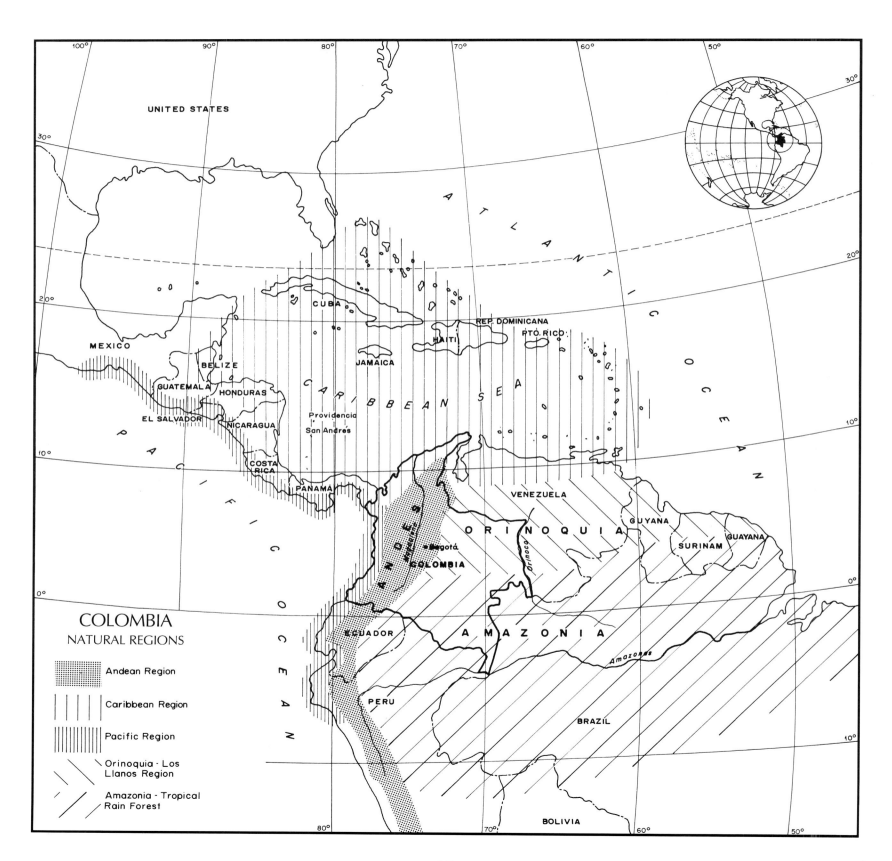

COLOMBIA
NATURAL REGIONS

Andean Region

Caribbean Region

Pacific Region

Orinoquia - Los
Llanos Region

Amazonia - Tropical
Rain Forest

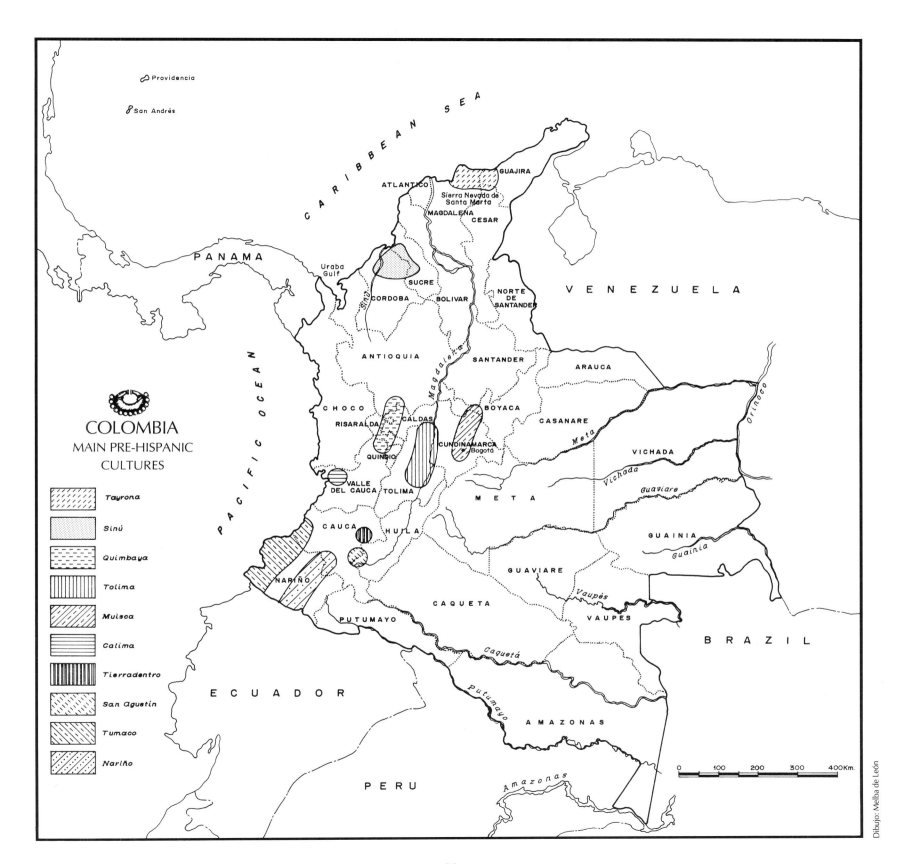

COLOMBIA
MAIN PRE-HISPANIC
CULTURES

Tayrona

Sinú

Quimbaya

Tolima

Muisca

Calima

Tierradentro

San Agustín

Tumaco

Nariño

Dibujo: Melba de León

INTRODUCTION

A legend of the Chibcha people, who lived for centuries in the Colombian Andes, tells of Bochica, a gray-haired sage dressed in a cotton tunic, who mysteriously appeared among the inhabitants. He taught them how to work the gold from their rivers into extraordinary objects, turn the earth from their mountains into bowls and statues, carve stone and wood into tools and sacred images, and weave themselves splendid garments and baskets. Before he left, Bochica carved the patterns for these crafts into the side of the mountains, lest his teachings be forgotten—and they have not.

The artifacts that remain today from the Chibcha and other ancient Colombian civilizations reveal a remarkable people—who built homes that could withstand the elements in the world's wettest rain forest, carved monumental statues of their ancestors and sacred spirits, and tantalized the western world with their golden objects set with the finest emeralds. Like Bochica's carvings, these artifacts serve not only as a testimony to the great achievements of cultures that disappeared long ago, but as patterns and inspirations for those who still live in the rain forests or snow-capped mountains of what is today Colombia.

Although little more is known of Bochica, it is clear from ancient remains that a highly sophisticated craft tradition flourished in Colombia long before the arrival of Christopher Columbus. (While the country is named after the explorer, it was not in fact Columbus, but his companion, Alonso de Ojeda, who made the first landing in 1499. Columbus never actually reached Colombia.) Tools have been found in the southern part of the country that date back sixty thousand years—nearly twice as far back as the earliest settlements found in North America. In the middle of the eighteenth century, along the valley of the Magdalena River, a Spanish monk discovered the remains of San Agustín, which, along with Tierradentro and Ciudad Perdida, is one of the most important archaeological sites in the Americas. Some time between the sixth century B.C. and the twelfth century A.D., its inhabitants carved hundreds of stone figures of their gods and ancestors. There were numerous other pre-Columbian civilizations—the Muisca, Quimbaya, Tolima, Tumaco, Nariño, Sinú, and Calima—however, few left behind such monuments, and most are best known for their gold and clay artifacts.

Ironically, it was these minute, golden artifacts that eventually brought disaster to the ancient people of Colombia. When the first Conquistadors arrived on the northern shores of the continent and were greeted by people who made such everyday items as dress pins and fishing hooks of gold, the explorers were sure that they had at last come upon El Dorado—land of the golden mountains. Rumors of an in-land culture whose religious rituals involved throwing a golden man and golden offerings into a sacred lake sent the Spanish deep into the country. But, it was with the inferior metal of their iron swords that the Spanish were able to quickly conquer these golden civilizations. Boats sailed to Spain laden with gold objects and emeralds, and returned to the Americas with more and more treasure-seekers, as well as Africans who were sold there as slaves. Missionaries soon followed, introducing Christianity to the aboriginal people and establishing settlements throughout the country.

After the Conquest, the Spanish crown ruthlessly colonized

and evangelized the inhabitants of the "New Granada." In 1812, Simón Bolívar, leading an impoverished army, undertook a long and heroic campaign to unify the states of South America. After years of fighting, Gran Colombia—Venezuela, Ecuador, Colombia, and Panama—won independence from Spain. But their union was short-lived and in 1830 the territories separated. In 1886, the Colombian constitution, which—with modifications—has served the country for more than a century, was written.

The population of the country today is fairly racially integrated, with most of the thirty million people of Indigenous-European, European-African, or Indigenous-African descent. About twenty-five percent of Colombians are of pure European, African, or Indigenous descent. The topography of the country is enormously varied—mountains and even a desert along the coast, plains to the northeast, and jungle to the southeast. And the country is rich in natural resources: Colombia is the world's primary supplier of emeralds, a gold exporter, the second largest producer of coffee, a major exporter of cut flowers and bananas, and a sugar producer.

The Colombian artisans of the past made use of all of nature's resources, transforming the often forbidding deserts, mountains, and jungles into habitable places through the creation of their utilitarian objects. This indomitable creativity still marks the craft world today. The craft industry in Colombia is, remarkably, a thriving one. It is strongest in regions where there are still substantial native populations—in the desert peninsula of Guajira in the north, along the Pacific Coast, in the southern Andes, and throughout the Amazon. Many of these communities still live in traditional ways and are thus the best

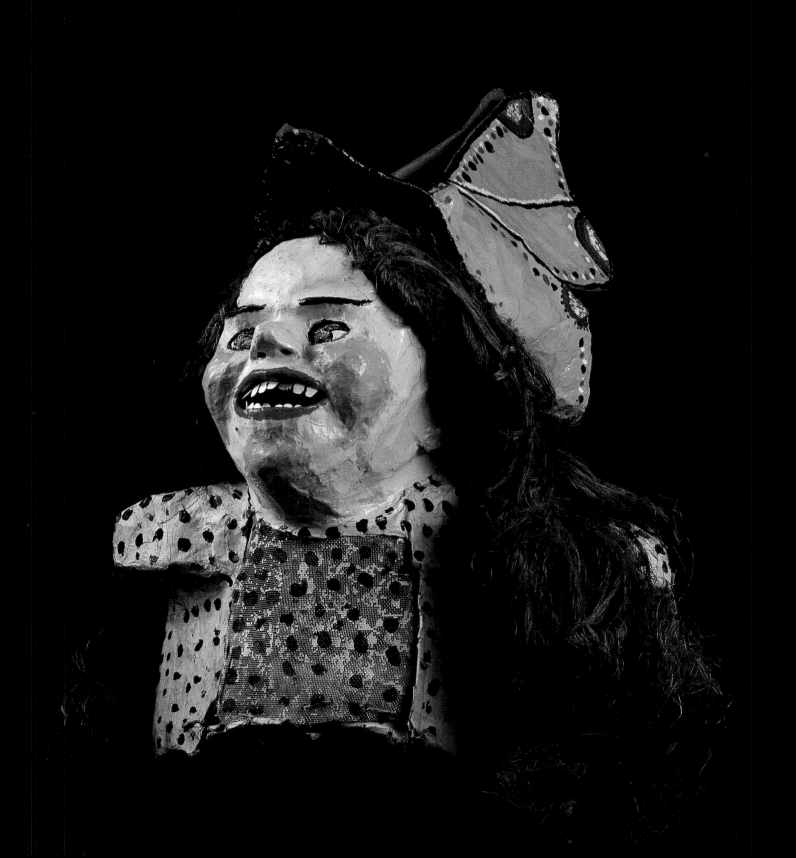

protectors of ancient craft traditions. Fortunately, over the last few years, movements to safeguard the privacy of these aboriginal people and preserve their lands from developers have attracted supporters and renewed interest in the cultural history of the country.

This book presents artifacts—or *artefactos*—from everyday life, objects that have accompanied Colombian people through the centuries, both in their earthly and spiritual activities. These include remnants of pre-Columbian civilizations, traditional indigenous creations, as well as those that bear the mark of many non-native cultures including Aztec, Maya, Inca, European, and African. In both English and Spanish, the word artifact means, literally, "made with skill or art." Although all worthy of museums, these are not just exhibition pieces, nor are their makers all members of a separate artisan class. There is no Colombian home, however humble, that does not have a handmade broom, stool, basket, textiles, or rustic furniture; nor is there a single Amazon Indian who cannot quickly piece together a basket from leaves found in the jungle. Many of the crafts made today still retain a significance beyond the strictly utilitarian, from the basketholder whose hourglass shape is a fertility symbol to the stool carved by a young man as a sign of his coming of age. But while these artifacts have survived for centuries, the gradual industrialization of the country—and increasing mass production of goods—poses a threat to the continuity of a craft tradition. This book is an attempt to document these crafts and introduce them to a wider industrialized world where similar traditions are vanishing.

18

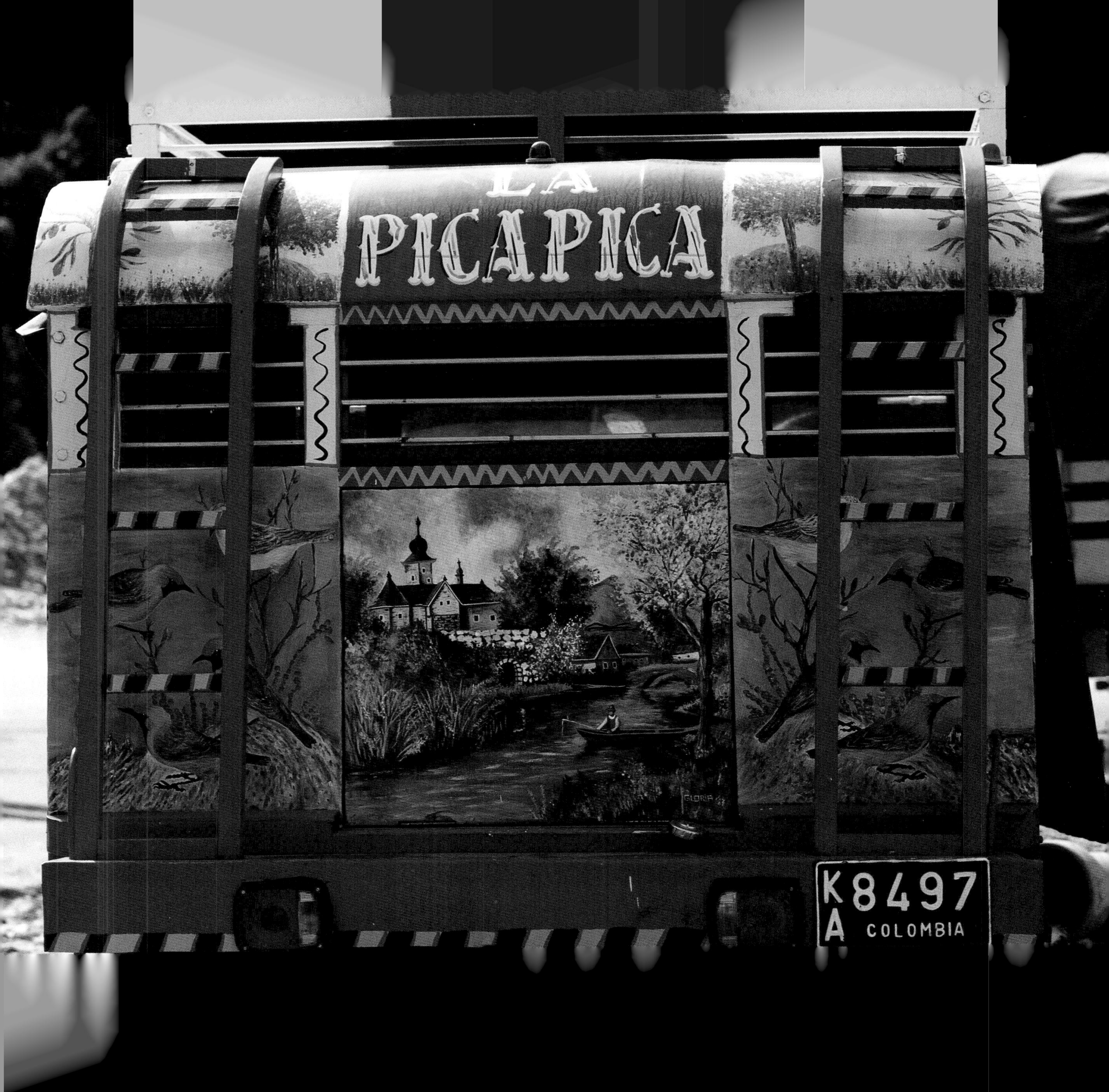
LA
PICAPICA
GLORIA
K 8497
A COLOMBIA

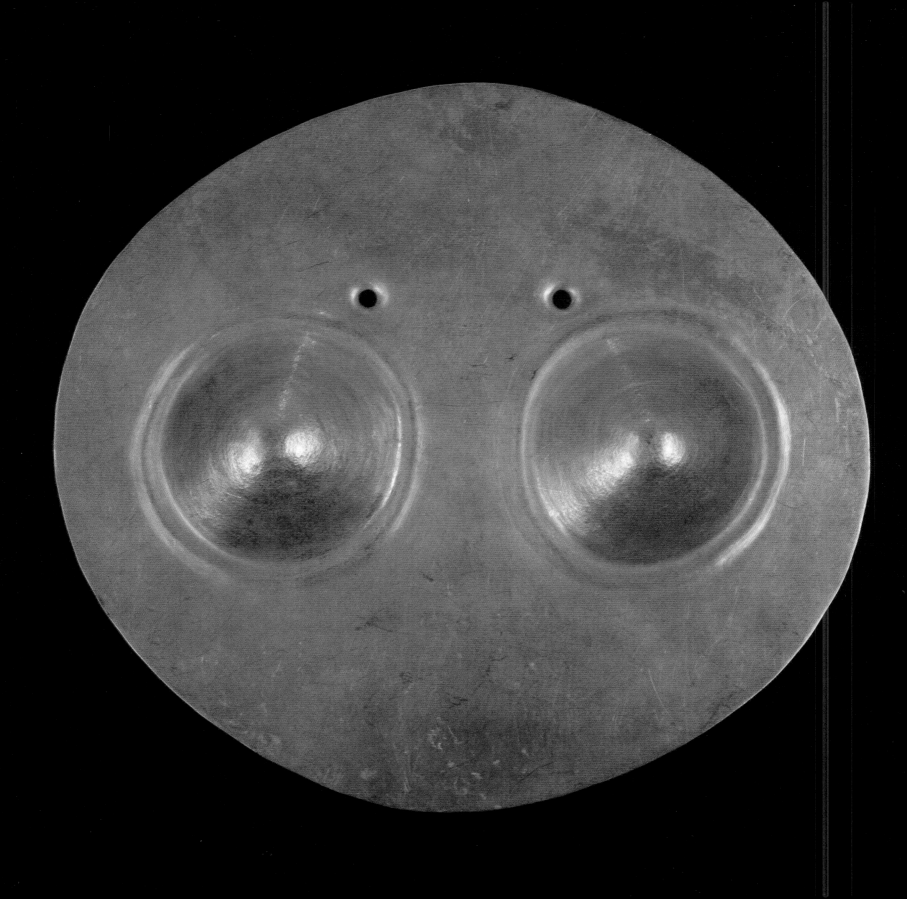

METAL

There is a theory that the ancient Greek prince Jason and his heroic Argonauts sailed not only throughout the Mediterranean, Aegean, and Black seas in their quest for the golden fleece of a winged ram, but that they in fact crossed the Atlantic and made it all the way to the northern coast of South America, and it was there that they found the magical fleece.

A study of the remarkable goldwork of Colombia makes it understandable that such a theory could ever have been formulated. Wherever the golden fleece was indeed found, however, the metalworkers of ancient Colombia achieved a level of craftsmanship that ranks among the highest in the world.

The first inhabitants of the area now known as Colombia settled around the best agricultural lands, in the valleys of the great rivers or foothills of the Andean chain, where there were also rich gold deposits. The principal centers for gold mining, then, were clustered in the valleys of the Magdalena, Cauca, Sinú, and Nechi rivers, as indicated by archaeological finds in these regions. Where the gold lay buried in subterranean veins it could be reached through narrow shafts dug deep into the earth. A much easier way to obtain the precious metal was discovered in soft riverbeds and sand pits. Large amounts of the metal could be gathered in a short time by sifting gravel from

Pre-Columbian gold pendant. A.D. III century. San Agustín culture.

Opposite. A golden, repoussé *breastplate. Such adornment was worn as protection in battle and as a sign of prestige during sacred ceremonies. A.D. X century. Sinú culture.*

the rivers until flecks of gold were visible in the bottom of the pan. This process is known as *barequeo*—or panning. The early *barequeros* also devised a system of canals, dug in the earth or made from bamboo chutes, that diverted the river's currents to terraces and sandy deposits where the panners could then flush out the gold. This technique, known as the canal or chute system, worked so efficiently that it soon spread from Colombia to other parts of America. It was later adopted by the Spaniards who continued to use the clever mining method.

Once the raw material was obtained, artisans would smelt the ore in small clay ovens, keeping the fire hot with wooden, bamboo, or clay blowpipes. Pre-Colonial metalwork is easily distinguished from later periods by the dominance of gold. The large number of gold deposits throughout the territory, the lack of technical knowledge for smelting iron, the scarcity of silver, and perhaps absence of tin explain why such a tremendous gold production developed.

While the various pre-Columbian peoples all devised their own styles and methods for working gold, they shared a distinctive gold culture. Thus, the goldworking tradition that lasted from approximately the third century before Christ to about the tenth century included the people of Tumaco, Calima, San Agustín, Tierradentro, Nariño, Tolima, and the finest of them all—the

Quimbaya. This earliest tradition is known for its pieces made from a pure gold (twenty-four karat), or an alloy made with a small percentage of copper. Molten gold was poured into shell, stone, or clay molds, which were often modeled into the shapes of local flora and fauna; or the metal was hammered over stone anvils with mallets into thin sheets of gold. The sheets were then embossed or assembled together with small tacks. Some of the goldsmiths, who lived in regions that were not as rich in gold, developed a system of oxidation to enhance the appearance of their less pure creations. The gold could be drawn to the surface of the object and the copper cleaned away.

These master pre-Columbian craftsmen made body adornments such as nose rings, nose plugs, diadems, ear cuffs, and helmets and breastplates that were worn as protection, in ceremonies, and to indicate rank. Utilitarian objects—such as *poporos* for carrying lye, small bottles, and bowls—were fashioned in gold, as well as totemic figurines whose stylized anthropomorphic and zoomorphic forms had ritualistic significance. It was primarily among the *cacicazgos*, or chieftain-ruled societies of the Andes that these sophisticated techniques were refined. Their social structures called for the existence of specialized craftsmen and artisan centers to provide tangible ways of denoting status and authority during social, political, and religious activities.

A golden vessel that once held a lime paste made from pulverized shells. A. D. V century. Calima culture.

By the tenth century, another goldworking tradition had emerged; this included the Sinú, Tayrona, and Muisca cultures—the last two of these survived until the time of the Conquest and it was their work that so tantalized the first Spanish Conquistadors. The procedures used by these metallurgists were similar to the earlier cultures except that they used a less pure gold and devised additional methods for working the metal, such as false filigree, gilding, and the lost-wax method. False filigree, or *falsa filigrana*, was a technique that could achieve an effect similar to filigree—an extraordinarily meticulous process of decorating with grains or beads of gold or silver—by using, instead, twisted and soldered wires. The Muiscas, who worked copper mines, devised a process of gilding copper with a thin surface of gold, which became known as *tumbaga*. The lost-wax method involved forming a desired shape out of wax and then covering it in clay. When the wax-and-clay object was fired, the wax would melt and drip out, leaving a hollow clay shell into which the gold could be poured.

The first Spanish in the area arrived along the northern Caribbean coast. Having conquered the New World's largest empire, that of the Aztecs, and exhausted the wealth of Montezuma's lands, the Spanish intensified their search for the origin of this wealth. They were spurred on by numerous tales describing places of extraordinary riches, golden objects such as those they had found among the Inca, and a legendary city of gold. This last image is what sent the Conquistadors plunging deep into Colombia, rather than keeping their explorations to the coast, as they had elsewhere on the continent. It was conjured up as a place whose splendor knew no equal in any realm; a city whose streets were paved in gold and led to an imperial palace where a valiant caste of Indians lived surrounded by their enormous treasure trove of gems and precious metals. The local inhabitants nodded when asked of this utopian civilization—El Dorado—always signalling further ahead, to a faraway place that one would reach after crossing the mountains and plains and jungles.

Along the way to El Dorado, the Conquistadors sacked towns and looted graves, stealing the countless goldworks that generations of Indians had buried with their dead. But these sacred objects were not enough, and driven by greed, the Spanish moved inland, in the hopes of discovering the gold mines themselves. Initially, they employed Indian labor, but this work force was decimated by disease and gradually replaced by enslaved Africans, who were brought to the Americas by the Spanish. Slavery continued in the region for four centuries—the duration of Spain's domination of South America.

According to official reports from the Spanish Colonial government, approximately one century

A pre-Columbian, bird-like breastplate cast in gold using the "lost-wax method" and hammering. A.D. IX century. Tolima culture.

A golden nose plug created by the ancient Tayrona, reflects their skill as metallurgists. A.D. X century. Tayrona culture.

after the Conquest had begun, one hundred and eighty tons of gold and sixteen thousand tons of silver were shipped to the Iberian peninsula. The entire colonizing process was, in one way or another, governed by the search for gold or the discovery of the principal mining centers.

Once the violence of the Conquest had ended, the Colonial period ensued and the process of populating territory and building a new society—made up now of the aboriginal population, as well as Spaniards, Africans, and *mestizos*—or those of mixed ancestry—arose. The artisan emerged as one of the key figures of this new culture. Spanish and Italian gold- and silversmiths arrived in the New Reign of Granada to orchestrate the development of a metal industry. The silver and golden objects were this time, however, not destined for tombs, ritual figures, or even jewelry—but were revamped for the Church and the Colonial homes of Spanish families. Gilded chalices, monstrances, lecterns, and chasubles embroidered with gold and silver threads were created alongside silver receptacles, stemware, platters, flatware, and decorative pieces that graced the salons of Spanish homes. Founded in 1600, Barbacoas was the largest gold-producing center in the New Reign of Granada until the middle of the nineteenth century.

Iron had already made its appearance in the New World in the form of weapons, armor, helmets, and horseshoes during the Conquest. And now, master craftsmen were brought from other parts of the new empire, especially Quito, in what is now Ecuador, where important metallurgic production centers had been formed, to teach the local craftsmen. The expertise of these men had actually been garnered from converted Moslems, who traveled with the Spanish armies. In Popayán, artisans soon discovered an expanding market for furniture, hardware, copper, and iron pieces. Workshops were established to produce rifles, lamps, and cannons, cast church bells, and practice the elegant art of inlay work.

Metallurgists also turned their craftsmanship to architectural elements. Iron was widely used for window railings, heavy church and convent doors, door knockers, locks, and great Gothic-style hinges. Delicate, wrought-iron gates, instead of front doors, marked the entrances to Colonial homes, allowing air to circulate more freely. In the Republican era, around the middle of the nineteenth century, the opening of the first ironworks broadened the use of metal, including, of course, as rails for the new railroad.

Copper stirrups and some troughs and vessels for home and decorative uses were also introduced to the country during the Colonial period. The manufacturing of copper and brass was concentrated in the town of Tibirita in Cundinamarca.

Gold pendants decorated in relief. A.D. I century. Tumaco culture.

Pre-Columbian gold earrings. A.D. XII century. Nariño culture.

Opposite. The remarkable face—forged in repoussé*— that looks out from this breast-plate wears the traditional ear and nose adornments of the ancient Colombians. A.D. V century. Calima culture.*

In the eighteenth century, the Baroque style flourished and lavish, exuberant creations began to emerge from Colombian workshops. Masterpieces of the goldsmith's art, such as the famous monstrance that Jesuit priests commissioned from Joseph Galaz, demonstrate the extraordinary talent of Colonial jewelers. Begun in 1700 and finished seven years later, this monstrance, encrusted with nearly fifteen hundred emeralds, has been named "La Lechuga" which means "Head of Lettuce"—after the dominant green color of the emeralds.

At the beginning of the nineteenth century, with the war for independence, foundries, metalsmiths, and artisans were forced to shift the output of their workshops. Military requirements imposed new demands on metallurgy. Aside from the large-scale production of bullets and cannon balls, there was a heightened demand for swords, scabbards, uniform buttons, medals to decorate the valiant, gold pins, harness ornaments, and insignias. The well-known Street of the Silversmiths in Santafé de Bogotá experienced a feverish period of activity, meeting the demands of the military, while still accommodating the civilian requests for hammered silver tableware, goblets, coffers, flatware, and candelabra.

The splendid creations of the sleepy Colonial town of Mompós were exalted in the 1920s when bananas were first exported in huge quantities and

brought wealthy foreign investors to the area. During the Second World War, Jewish immigrants came to live in the village and renewed the ancient goldworking traditions. One of the traditional secular uses of gold was the renowned filigree of Mompós. Golden threads are made thinner and thinner, using rudimentary equipment, until they have the thickness of a human hair. Then, these fine threads are braided and twisted in spirals, winding the golden thread around frames that come in many different shapes, limited only by the artisan's imagination. Necklaces from Mompós, as well as brooches and earrings, subtly evoke the exuberant flora of the tropics.

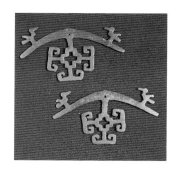

Golden, pre-Columbian earrings. A.D. XII century. Nariño culture.

Opposite. This golden snail was made as a religious offering, probably intended to be thrown into one of the Muisca's sacred Andean lakes. The Muisca lived from about the first to the sixteenth century near what is today Bogotá, the capital of Colombia. When the early Conquistadors learned of the remarkable Muisca rituals, involving the ablution of a "golden man" and gold objects into sacred waters, they took off in search of this lakeside "kingdom of gold." Ironically, gold was not actually mined in this region, but was obtained by the Muisca through trade with other peoples. A.D. IX century. Muisca culture.

The goldwork of Colombia today—like all of its crafts—has been influenced by numerous cultures, beginning, of course, with its own indigenous, pre-Columbian ones, then by the conquering Spanish and the Arabs in their armies, other Europeans, as well as Africans brought over initially as slaves to mine the metals.

Today's Colombian jewelers explore these age-old traditions, bringing to them a modern eye. Some jewelers have renounced contemporary styles completely, adhering instead to the designs from cultures of the past. With alloys that resemble the gold produced by those ancient societies, they create near perfect replicas of jewelry manufactured by pre-Columbian masters.

Pre-Columbian fishhooks, tupus (pins used to hold women's shawls in place), chisels, needles, and tweezers—all fashioned in a pure, high-karat gold.

Early in the 1500s, when the first Spanish arrived along the northwest coast of Colombia and saw that the local Indians made such everyday objects as tweezers and needles out of gold, they became convinced that they were at the threshold of the legendary El Dorado—a kingdom of golden mountains. While the everyday use of gold was, indeed, quite natural to the Indians, they also prized its beauty highly and used it as well in their most sacred rituals. In general, objects of this kind, made from the first century A.D. to the sixteenth century by the Quimbaya, Tayrona, Calima, and Tolima cultures, are found in tombs, although the fishhooks have been discovered on riverbanks.

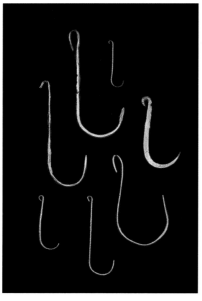

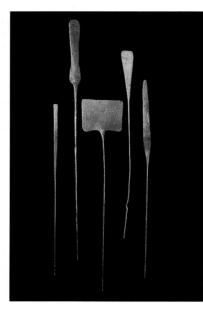

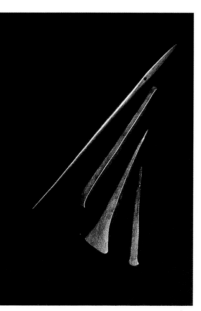

Opposite. By hammering a thin sheet of gold inside the hard, rounded base of a calabash shell, a Quimbaya goldsmith wrought this elegant but simple ceremonial bowl.
The metalwork of the Quimbaya, who lived along the gold-rich Cauca River, is considered to be the finest—both technically and stylistically—in South America. A.D. XI century.
Quimbaya culture.

The lightly etched spoon is a creation of the Calima people, who lived about one hundred miles to the south of the Quimbaya, also along the shores of the Cauca. A.D. XI century. Calima culture.

Right. The striking designs and meticulous methods of the country's first metalworkers have been perpetuated by Colombia's jewelers today, as these contemporary pieces in gold and semi-precious stones illustrate.

The spiralling circle, seen again and again in the work of pre-Hispanic jewelers for whom it signified infinity, is still a favored motif among artisans. As well, the rather unusual, bilateral shapes of the nose plugs that were worn as symbols of status by the most ancient of South American people, have been transformed here into pendants, brooches, and earrings.

Jewelers continue to hammer out golden forms in an ancient process—repoussé—used by most early civilizations. They also still cast metal in the "lost-wax method," an elaborate procedure in which one first covers a wax model with a substance such as clay, and then heats the assemblage until the wax has melted and drained out of small holes in the clay. The hollowed clay form is then filled with gold or another molten metal. Such attention to ancient traditions has helped to preserve the cultural heritage of the early inhabitants of the continent. G. Cano, Bogotá.

Opposite.
Left. For over two hundred years, until the middle of the nineteenth century, Barbacoas was the goldworking capital of Colombia. Using the sophisticated mining and purification techniques of the pre-Columbians, goldworkers from this town at the southernmost tip of the country, created a splendid array of golden objects. Artisans here today continue to work in a high-karat, almost pure gold, with a minimum amount of silver or copper, such as that used by their ancestors centuries ago. These gold necklaces and earrings are set with precious stones. Flower petals, butterfly wings, and other motifs have been outlined in gold filigree. Barbacoas, Nariño.

Top right. Emilio Cortés in his jewelry workshop. On the table before him lie many of the implements of his trade: pliers, pincers, anvils, gourds, boxes, jars for use in the chemical processing of metals, and a set of scales. He weighs the gold, first after cleaning, then after alloying, and once again when the piece is finished. He uses a small, rudimentary stove and bellows to melt the gold. Gems are soldered on at the very end of the process with a blowtorch. Barbacoas, Nariño.

Bottom right. Jewelers of Mompós specialize in filigree work—an exquisite use of gold thread that resembles the delicacy of lace. Mompós, Bolívar.

Opposite. A flourishing gold and silverworking industry developed in Colombia during the Colonial era, due in part to the flamboyant, Baroque tastes of the Europeans at the time and the need for ecclesiastical furnishings for the churches of the New World and those at home. This monstrance is one of the most spectacular examples of ecclesiastic goldwork in Colombia. It is called La Lechuga, or The Lettuce, because of the dominant green of its extraordinary 1,435 emeralds from the Muzo, Coscuez, Chivor, and Somondoco mines. The emeralds of Colombia are considered the finest in the world. The consecrated Host is kept in the upper part of the monstrance, in the form of the sun. A golden angel supports the vessel from beneath. The sun is twelve and one half inches in diameter and the entire monstrance is thirty one inches high. XVIII century. Bogotá.

Top left. While the design of this eighteen-karat gold necklace-bracelet set is contemporary, the techniques used to cut and shape the sodalite (blue) and crystal emeralds date back to pre-Columbian times. G. Cano, Bogotá.

Bottom left. Inspired by pre-Columbian goldwork, the matching neck piece, earrings, and ring are set with smooth-cut, cabochon emeralds and multi-faceted brilliants. The eighteen-karat gold foundation contains about seventy-five percent pure gold. (Twenty-four karat gold is absolutely pure.) G. Cano, Bogotá.

Following pages.
Page 36. In the seventeenth and eighteenth centuries, most of the gold available was reserved for use on ecclesiastical furnishings. However, equally splendid items for domestic use—as well as for the Church—were cast in silver. This silverware set was hammered and assembled using the techniques of Colonial Colombia. Alonso Arte, Bogotá.

Page 37. Little zoomorphic figures—perhaps remnants of a pre-Christian culture—have been soldered onto this silver holy water vessel and aspergillum. Popayán, one of the earliest Spanish settlements, became an important religious and commerce center as it was located along the "gold route." XVIII century. Popayán, Cauca.

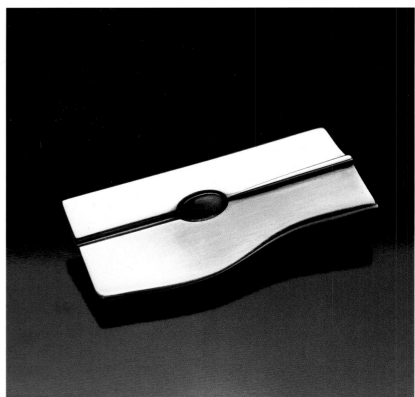

Opposite. Jewelry-making continues today to be one of the finest of Colombian crafts. These silver brooches are set with zircons and "tiger's-eyes"; the figure at top right also includes eighteen-karat gold. J. A. Roda, Nuri Carulla, Bogotá.

Left. The Guambiano Indians, who live in small mountain communities in southwestern Colombia, crafted these silver necklaces inset with semi-precious stones. One can see, in the cross-like pendants, how the Christian motifs introduced by the Spanish have been combined with pre-Hispanic metalworking traditions. Silvia, Cauca.

Right. During the Colonial period, Tibirita, an Andean town in central Colombia, earned renown for its production of large-scale metal objects—church bells, cauldrons, pots—which were in demand by the Spaniards. Fashioned in a traditional European style, these shoe-shaped stirrups—known as Moorish stirrups—were particularly useful in protecting a rider's feet along the narrow bridle paths and mountain roads of the Colombian countryside. Early XIX century. Tibirita, Cundinamarca.

Opposite. Bronze pestles and mortars decorated with relief-work and incision. XVIII and XIX centuries. Bogotá.

The use of copper as a basic material for utilitarian and decorative objects, as well as the techniques for working it, were introduced to Colombia by the Spanish. Traditionally, the copper was modeled by continuous hammering until it achieved the shape of the desired object. Today, however, most craftsmen begin with ready-made, thin sheets of metal, which they then beat to imitate the hammering effect.

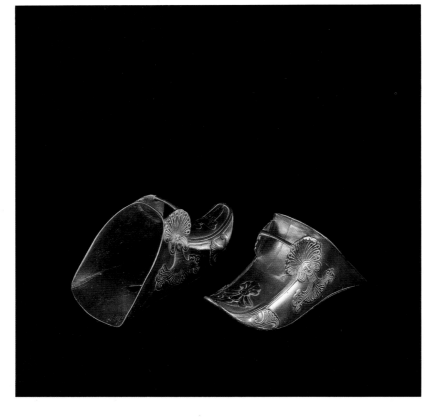

Above. Large bronze pans are used in sugar cane mills for processing brown sugar. Sugar is one of the main agricultural products of Colombia. Rosas, Cauca.

Opposite. This enormous brass vessel has been decorated and strengthened with threads of the same alloy; woven handles are attached at either side. Although a contemporary creation, its form is inspired by pre-Columbian pottery. Bogotá.

Following pages. A pattern has been etched onto this decorative copper frieze with acid. Marcelo Villegas, Manizales, Caldas.

46

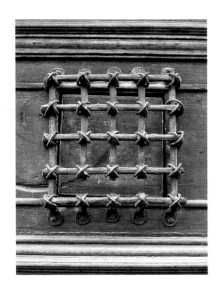

Above. Situated on the northern, Caribbean coast of Colombia, Cartagena was settled early on by the Spaniards and retains today a strong Spanish flavor in its architecture and ornamentation, such as this rivetted-iron window grille. Cartagena, Bolívar.

Left.
Top. Detail of a wrought-iron grille. Marcelo Villegas, Manizales, Caldas.

Bottom. Ornate leafy sprigs, typical of this coffee-growing region, adorn this wrought-iron grille. Genaro Mejía, Manizales, Caldas.

Right. A wrought-iron gate divides the entrance of this Colonial house from the patio. The development of iron-working techniques during the Colonial period, particularly in Mompós and Popayán, led to wonderfully imaginative architectural ornamentation. XVIII century. Popayán, Cauca.

Left. Contemporary wrought-iron seat made by applying layers of bronze and copper over iron. Taller de Forja Catalana, Popayán, Cauca.

Opposite. Wrought-iron bedstead with copper appliqué work. XIX century. Popayán, Cauca.

Above. Polished iron and brass wall lamp. Guillermo Arias, Bogotá.

Left. Polished iron and brass lamp and candlesticks. Guillermo Arias, Bogotá.

Opposite. Contemporary hammered and polished vessel in copper and silver alloy. Juana Méndez, Bogotá.

CLAY

Pottery is one of the most enduring marks of a civilization. While it is not always the first material creation of a culture, it is often the only remnant of the culture's existence and so of enormous archaeological importance. The ceramic remains of a people can reveal the approximate time-frame during which they lived and provide insights into their technology, artistry, religion, and possible commercial ties with neighboring people—for, as we will see, clay was not just limited to domestic wares but was modeled into votive offerings, buried as part of funerary rites, and shaped into adobe bricks, which, when dried in the sun became an important building material.

The oldest pottery found in Colombia dates from about 3500 B.C.; this was discovered alongside stone artifacts in Puerto Hormiga, on the northern coast of the country. By the end of the second millennium B.C., a sedentary farming community is thought to have been established along the Caribbean coast, as ceramic remains have also been discovered there.

Kaolin—a fine white clay, creta—a chalky substance, and black, red, and yellow clays are all found abundantly in the lands along Colombia's many rivers and mountainsides; the pre-Columbian cultures who settled these regions possess an extensive ceramic record. They produced pottery for numerous purposes by using

A pre-Columbian clay amphora. A.D. 1250. Nariño culture.

Opposite. Ceramic burial urns; the effigies on the lids represent the spirits of the deceased. A.D. XI century. Various cultures from Tamalameque, Mosquito, and Bajo Magdalena. Alonso Arte, Bogotá.

manufacturing and decorating techniques common to most early civilizations. In ancient Colombia, as today, pottery was generally made by women, who, until the advent of the wheel, either spiralled thin rolls of clay on top of one another, smoothing out the ribs to create a strong, flat surface; or pressed soft clay into shells or other hard forms; occasionally, they spun a circular dish around by hand, and formed a bowl or plate on top of it in a concept similar to the potter's wheel. But even within these shared methods, some differences in specific form and decoration have been determined from one ancient culture to another. Based on these differences, scientists have been able to establish varying degrees of technological development and variations of social and religious patterns.

The ancient cultures of the Tumaco, Nariño, Muisca, Quimbaya, Calima, Sinú, and Tayrona, who lived throughout the western part of Colombia, were elaborate in their ceramic expression. Religious, mythical, and magical representations were integrated into everyday objects. Though much of their pottery was made to serve utilitarian functions, the inventory of festive and ceremonial objects, such as statuary and musical instruments, was considerable. Beside pots, ewers, amphoras, cups, and vessels, whistles, panpipes, flutes, and funerary urns have been found by gravesites, among the remains of homes, or in ceremonial sites, such as the sacred lakes of the Muiscas.

The fertility cults of the Tumaco, one of the most ancient of the Colombian cultures, is evident in the erotic nature of the pottery produced by their artisans. The remarkable pottery of the Nariño people, who lived in the southern Andes, was particularly fine; it is recognizable for its lavishly painted and decorated surfaces that bear the influence of earlier cultures to the south. The ceramics of the Muisca, on the other hand, were generally plain, with lovely shapes but little surface decoration. Both they and the Quimbaya lavished more attention on their goldwork, although their ceramic production was still significant. The Calima flourished at the crossroads of several cultures and their ceramics, which are often zoomorphic in shape, show the influence of varied peoples. Sinú pottery appears to have been largely utilitarian, made from a cream-colored clay that was then decorated in red. The Tayrona made ceremonial ceramics in black clay, funerary urns in cream clay, and domestic wares in red clay.

The arrival of the Spanish Conquistadors at the close of the fifteenth century brought about some major changes in the development of Colombia's ceramic production. Many of the ancient traditions ceased altogether as the native inhabitants were forced to flee or were killed. Those that did survive colonization were

Pre-Columbian ceramic stamps were rolled upon cloth, tree bark, or even human skin to leave behind a trail of repeated patterns. The bottom image shows such a stamp in use for textile design. Quimbaya culture.

introduced to new techniques brought over from Europe, including the potter's wheel, which had not before been used by the indigenous people of the Americas. With the introduction of the wheel, vessels could be made with more uniformity and speed—although the pre-Hispanic methods are still commonly used throughout the country today. The Spanish also brought over kilns that reached much higher temperatures than the Indian ovens or custom of "sun drying" and thus could produce stronger ceramics. And they taught methods of vitrification or glazing; the early potters of the region had previously tinted their ceramics with natural dyes or burnished the unfired surfaces to produce a sheen. In fact, like the clay remains of ancient Colombia, the ceramics of Colombia today can reveal a great deal about their makers. Where the Spanish presence was strongest, one finds potters making wares clearly influenced by European techniques. Thus, while ceramic production continued during and after the Conquest—and in many ways, was improved by the newly learned techniques—the tradition that had been inherited from indigenous ancestors became profane rather than sacred or ritualistic and was turned to imminently utilitarian purposes.

Geographic isolation, however, saved some of Colombia's indigenous population from the devastating embrace of colonization, and these people, such as the Emberá, Tucano, Kogui, and

Tunebo communities, have preserved their ancient ceramic traditions. While the pottery of the Emberá of Chocó appears to be strictly utilitarian—such as the *cántaro* used to roast corn, the *kuru* for cooking a corn-based soup, and the *choko* for storing a fermented corn liquor—the forms and materials of these pieces are all imbued with magical-religious significance and indicate how daily life among such cultures is inextricably linked to the spiritual life. In recent years, however, the Emberá added to their repertoire to accommodate tourists and newer settlers. Potters now produce flowerpots, ovenware, ashtrays, and candlesticks. According to anthropological studies, of the thirteen types of ceramic containers produced by the Emberá community, six belong to their ancient traditions and seven to modern innovation. The material culture of the indigenous peoples of the jungles of the Amazon and the Vaupés region, such as the Tucano, includes both utilitarian and ritualistic pottery. The Tucano use a ceremonial ceramic cup when imbibing *yajé* (a sacramental hallucinogen). The cup is decorated with complex figurative motifs that turn iridescent white, yellow, and red during the participants hallucinogenic "visions." To the Tucano, the colors signify masculine and feminine powers, fertilization and gestation, and the cup itself represents the place where gestation occurs. The spiritual leaders of the Koguī, descendants of the

A contemporary clay kiln for processing gold. Ráquira, Boyacá.

Ceramic ocarinas—simple wind instruments. A.D. XII–XV century. Nariño culture.

Tayrona, make cone-shaped vessels with two handles for religious rituals. The Tunebo work five different types of vessels: three of them decorated and used for serving food, carrying water, and fermenting liquids; the other two are left undecorated and are for cooking and toasting coca leaves.

For centuries Ráquira in the department of Boyacá has been a famous ceramic production center. Raw materials here can be extracted from large veins of crumbly, chalky lime and kaolin found in the region.

The potters of Boyacá have carried on the traditions of their ancestors, the Muisca, using dense black clay with a high coal content, red clay with iron oxide, and white and yellow clays. But even here, techniques and styles have evolved over the centuries and today's creations result from a mixture of both native and European cultures, creating an amalgam that now has its own flavor. In addition to Ráquira, artisans in Sáchica and Sutamerchán make different-sized and proportioned receptacles, large pots and pitchers, basins, bowls, and unglazed chocolate pots for home use that are decorated with a paste called *chica*. In Chiquinquirá, Tausa, and Nemocón, artisans still manufacture ancient *moyos*—immense pots, which pre-Columbian societies used for refining salt from the nearby mines.

An interesting range of ceramics has survived in the department of Santander, in the towns of Guane and El Socorro, which were outside the influence of the Chibcha, the largest linguistic group of ancient Colombia. Pots with little necks, basins with handles on the edges, and round pots with vertical edges and horizontal handles are but a few examples of these distinctive designs.

In the department of Huila, ceramicists from Pitalito are well known for their delightful interpretations of country life in the Colombian Andes. *Chivas*—open, wooden-sided buses painted bright colors—are a common means of transportation, and the artisans of Pitalito have immortalized the *chiva* in replicas of these vehicles, overflowing with people, animals, and produce. In addition to *chivas,* street scenes, storefronts, marketplaces, and many other miniature representations of everyday life are rendered in minute detail and brilliant colors.

On the Atlantic Coast are many small, centuries-old ceramic production centers. The people of the small villages of the lower Magdalena River are especially talented. In this region, as in most of Colombia, the women make the pottery and tend to the children and homes while the men fish and farm. Pottery in the Guajira is simple and utilitarian, as is the rest of the material culture of these desert people. Most of the objects produced are utensils needed for

Artisans of the small town of Carmen produce these delightful plates, whose patterns are inspired by the local landscape and flora. Carmen de Viboral, Antioquia.

Opposite. Pre-Columbian vessels made in the brown clay found along the Cauca River. A.D. VIII century. Quimbaya culture.

domestic use. The result is an immediate response to immediate need. Even here, however, a certain ornamental character is clear.

After the arrival of the Spanish in South America, the red-brick and tiled Spanish-Moorish style of architecture—known as Mudéjar—was popularized in Colombia. Tiny Colonial settlements gradually developed into cities with distinctive architectural expressions. Clay-tiled roofs and brick facades appeared on houses, convents, churches, barracks, and other civic buildings. Soon indigenous inventions, such as adobe bricks, stone walls, and thatched roofs— depending upon the region—were added to the dominant features of Spanish Colonial architecture, creating an authentic style. In rural areas of the Andean high plains, in the departments of Cundinamarca, Boyacá, Nariño, and Cauca, one can still find these building styles today.

Curved, interlocking red roof tiles were an ever-present feature of the buildings erected during the reign of the viceroys of New Granada from the sixteenth to nineteenth centuries. These graceful, rough-textured tiles were used throughout Colombia and the Spanish Colonial empire to create the characteristic red, slanted rooftops. Apart from their decorative appearance, roof tiles are actually ideal for tropical climates, as rain can easily run down their tiny canals into roof

gutters—also made of clay, a material readily available in all regions.

Quite often brick was mixed with stone to erect walls. Innumerable Colonial country houses provide examples of this type of architecture. The central courtyard was enclosed on two or three sides, with arches in brick or stone, supported by stone columns on the lower floor and horizontal lintels on the upper floors. The cloistered halls were paved with large ceramic tiles, or perhaps brick or stone. Access to the interior part of the house was through a wide hallway that opened onto the middle of the courtyard.

Contemporary ceramic vessels—a new interpretation of the ancient coil method. Potters Cooperative, Chía, Cundinamarca.

Rolls of clay woven in basket-like fashion. Tatiana Montoya, Tabio, Cundinamarca.

Opposite. These elegant, double-spouted vessels with bridge handles were made for storing liquids. A.D. X century. Quimbaya culture.

From the Conquest forward, brick has been an inseparable component of urban development in Colombia, and, to a great degree, has dictated the progression of its architectural styles. Toward the end of the nineteenth century, industrial brickworks became essential elements of urban progress. And despite the fact that it is now called an industry, bricks continue to be manufactured by craftsmen in tile factories; the methods, still used by artisans, are inherited from the Colonial period. Like the potter's wheel and the European kiln, these new techniques were adapted to the needs and tastes of the native Colombians.

Previous pages. Rain and river water, filtered through these containers, is converted into potable water. These huge vessels are made of clay mixed with minerals and resins and fired at very high temperatures, which results in an extremely hard but porous substance. From left to right, they are Colonial, pre-Columbian, and contemporary. Bogotá, Tumaco culture, and Ráquira, Boyacá, respectively.

Pre-Columbian ceramic vessels. These pre-Columbian bowls are examples of wax-resist or "negative" painting. After applying patterns in hot wax to the surface of the fired bowl, the artisan dipped the piece in a colored clay slip, leaving only the unwaxed areas to absorb the color. The wax burned away during a second firing and the result was a contrasting pattern or design. A.D. XII–XV century. Different cultures.

Ceramic vessels stacked for drying. Before the vessels are fired in kilns, they are dried in the open air. During this phase the craftsmen polish them, smooth them with pieces of calabash to reduce porosity, or add handles—depending on their intended use. When each piece is white and dry, it is dampened slightly, then decorated. In the foreground is a box of miniature pieces called maíz tostado, *which include crockery, whistles, and animal figurines. They were originally part of ancient Chibcha rituals and are today bought by pilgrims as souvenirs of their visits to religious sanctuaries. Rubiano Family, Ráquira, Boyacá.*

Eva Villanueva making a clay vessel by hand. She began with a small, indented ball of clay, which she placed on a plate that can be spun around by hand. From this initial stage she gradually built the walls by coiling rolled strips of clay around the edge of the base and then stretching them upwards, while slowly spinning the plate to achieve a symmetrical result. Other methods used in Colombia are the potter's wheel, which was introduced by the Spanish, and molding—that is, either pouring clay inside a mold or shaping it around the outside of a mold. Ráquira, Boyacá.

Opposite.
Top left. The department of Boyacá, in the center of Colombia, is known for its splendid crafts, particularly its pottery from the town of Ráquira. This little clay horse, used here as a "piggy bank," has become one of the symbols of the pottery production of the region. It is often seen loaded with pots, firewood, or carrying a rider. Ráquira, Boyacá.

Top right. Ceramic "piggy bank" in the shape of a hen. Ráquira, Boyacá.

Bottom left. Ceramic teapots decorated in relief with stylized animal figures and scenes based on local mythology. Ráquira, Boyacá.

Bottom right. Clay vessels. Ráquira, Boyacá.

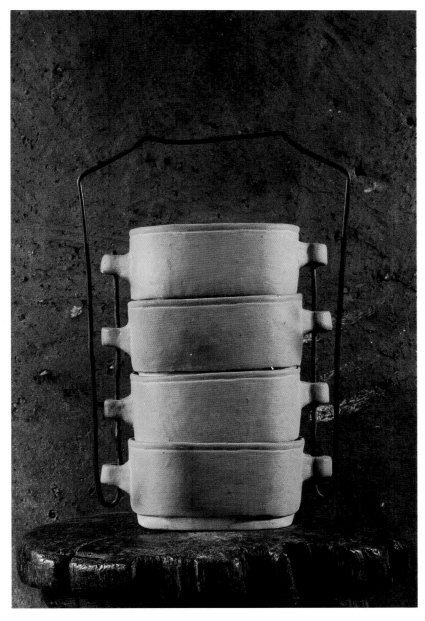

Left. These ceramic food containers can be tightly stacked, one on top of the other, to retain heat. Ráquira, Boyacá.

In Ráquira, the production of crafts is divided into urban and rural styles. The rural pottery is generally utilitarian; pots, large earthenware jars, and bowls for chocolate are standard fare. In the urban sector, artisans produce more decorative pottery, such as bells, lamps, and figurines for nativity crèches—a popular Colombian tradition. Local village scenes, churches, and a variety of animals figures are also made in urban workshops.

Top left. This is a traditional Colombian version of the European kiln. It has a high, open chamber made of adobe bricks and earthenware, topped by a chimney. Ráquira, Boyacá.

Bottom left. Water vessels are essential to the nomadic Wayuu Indians of northeastern Colombia, who live in the desert peninsula of Guajira. Wayuu Indians, Guajira.

Opposite. Potters from this region produce tiny clay vessels to sell alongside their ordinary household crockery in village markets. There are as many as thirty differently shaped "minatures," which are bought for decoration or given as gifts. Pottery in Colombia is generally made and decorated by women. La Capilla, Cundinamarca.

Opposite. Ceramic pots, known as moyos, in a range of shapes and sizes for plants, storing grains, or holding water and liquors. Because they are so large—some are over six feet high—they are made from several slabs of clay. Zipaquirá, Cundinamarca.

Top left and right. A cockfight and bullfight—two popular Colombian pastimes—in glazed ceramics. Chiquinquirá, Boyacá.

Left. Glazed pottery on sale in a village market. Chiquinquirá, Boyacá.

Among the raw materials used for these ceramic glazes are burnt copper, copper oxide, sulphur, lead, and ground marble—all diluted in water. The already fired vessels are submerged in the glaze and re-fired with or without applied decoration. The process of glazing makes the otherwise porous clay impermeable. The craftsmen of Ráquira frequently vary the effects of the glazes by manipulating the firing temperatures.

Above left and right. Utilitarian objects made from red and black clay found in the region. La Chamba, Tolima.

Opposite. Burnishing—or continuously rubbing—unfired clay can be as effective in adding a sheen as glazing, as this fruit bowl illustrates. Eduardo Sandoval, La Chamba, Tolima.

The ceramic tradition in the valley of La Chamba dates back to pre-Hispanic times. The products of this region include a wide range of domestic articles, which are fired in open bonfires on the ground, rather than in kilns. The local clays are red and black; the black clay is more common. The potters burnish their vessels with river stones before firing; this hardens the surface of the vessel and gives it a polished finish.

Opposite.
Top left. Stoneware teapots and
a coffeepot. Ronald Duncan,
Galería Deimos, Bogotá.

Top right. Clay vessel made
on a potter's wheel and fired
at a high temperature.
Ronald Duncan, Bogotá.

Bottom left. A drum made of
clay, leather, and woven
pita fibers. Ana María Botero,
Tabio, Cundinamarca.

Bottom right. This footed ceramic
dish is used to bake cassava bread,
a cracker or griddle-cake made
from the root of the bitter cassava
or manioc plant. The dough is
baked and then left out to cool on
rooftops. Cassava bread is the
basic food of the indigenous
people from Los Llanos and the
Amazon. Vaupés.

Left. Drum of clay and leather,
held taught with pita fibers. Drums
and panpipes are important
features of traditional Andean
music. Ana María Botero, Tabio,
Cundinamarca.

Following pages. Models of
churches from the high Andean
plateaux. The inside walls of these
pieces are sculpted with heads of
saints. Catholicism, which was
introduced by Spanish
missionaries, is the dominant
religion of the country, even in the
most remote mountain towns.
María Otilia Jerez, Ráquira,
Boyacá.

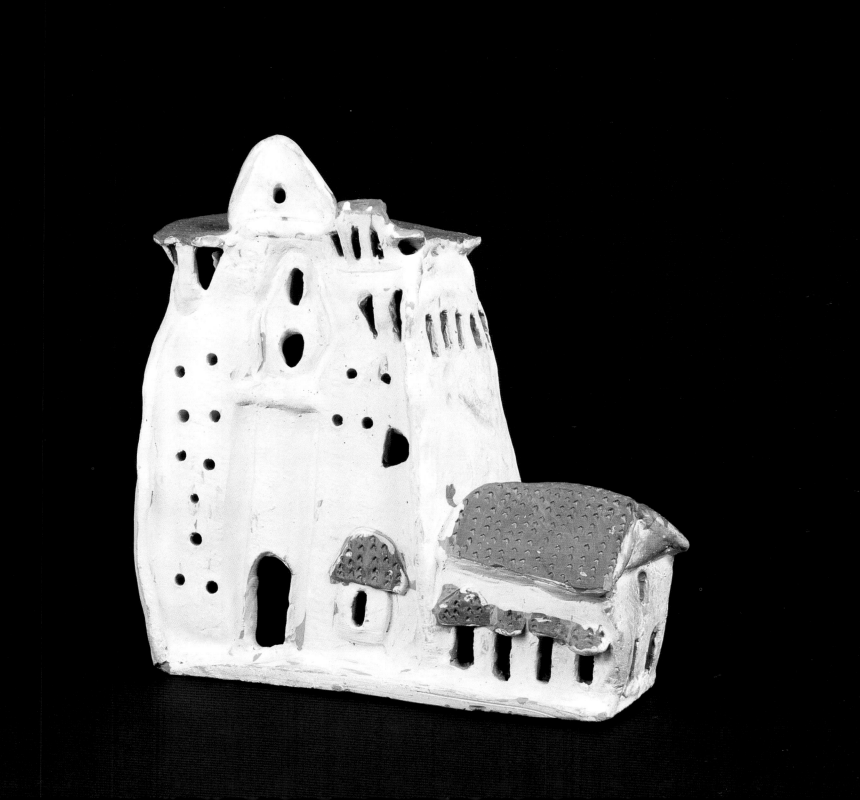

Above. A funerary procession depicted in clay. From the pre-Columbian burial urns to such sculptures as this, one can learn the significance of funerary ceremonies to the people of Colombia. Teodolindo Ovalle, Ráquira, Boyacá.

Below. A festive wedding celebration on top of a bus. This clay vignette is actually a typical Colombian scene; buses, brimming with people, parcels, and livestock are common sights in rural Colombia. The service is often irregular so passengers cannot afford to let a crowded bus pass by. Cecilia Vargas, Pitalito, Huila.

Opposite. Ceramic nativity scene. Cecilia Vargas, Pitalito, Huila.

In both Ráquira and further south in Pitalito, artisans make pottery inspired by their astute observations of daily life: they portray village market scenes, sporting events, marriages, religious processions, and feast days. Thus the ceramics become not only contemporary artifacts but also historical records of an age and culture.

Following page. Glazed ceramic tiles showing an array of musicians and dancers. La Mesa, Cundinamarca.

Left. The dome of San Ignacio Church in brick and glazed clay tiles. Jesuit missionaries began building this church in Bogotá early in the seventeenth century, but it was not completed until 1767. Bogotá.

Opposite.
Top. Details of brick courses and stacked clay tiles. Medellín, Bogotá, and La Esperanza, Caldas.

Bottom. A brick-laid street in a residential section of Bogotá.

Pre-Columbian Indians traditionally built their homes and public structures out of plant fibers and wood, and this building method is still kept up to some degree today. But when the Spanish arrived and introduced clay bricks and tiles as a new means of construction, it was soon absorbed into the pre-existing clay culture and became a standard building material, as well as the basis for a successful Colombian industry.

Above. Wax-polished brick floor and vaulted, tiled, Colonial roof. XVIII century. Casa del Márquez de San Jorge, Bogotá.

Opposite. Brickworks for production by the traditional technique. Dos Quebradas, Risaralda.

STONE

In 1757, Father Juan de Santa Gertrudis, a Spanish monk traveling along the Magdalena River that begins in the Macizo Colombiano Mountains, came upon one of the most extraordinary sites of the ancient world. A civilization that had flourished along the river's canyon centuries before had disappeared, leaving behind hundreds of monolithic stone carvings—humanlike figures, monsters, and animals. These massive statues were apparently funereal artifacts, part of the elaborate ancestral cults of their makers—and while their meaning remains a mystery to historians and archaeologists, they are a magnificent introduction to Colombia's stone culture.

The craft of masonry is as old as civilization. All pre-Columbian civilizations used stone; in fact, the first tools, weapons, and utensils made by the continent's earliest cultures were of stone. It was also stone that provided the basic material with which primitive cultures built their first temples and altars to rustic deities. Later on they learned how to carve stone, and through this discovery, opened a wide range of possibilities. From small scrapers, jewelry, and household wares, to the monumental statuary of San Agustín, the use of stone was associated with a broad group of domestic and ceremonial activities.

Among pre-Columbian cultures, the art of three populations stands out for their astounding use of

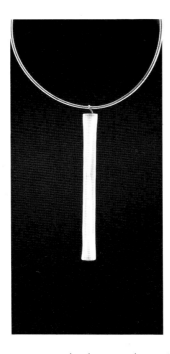

A pre-Columbian pendant made of hollowed, polished quartz, hanging from a modern silver necklace. Tayrona culture.

Opposite. Ancient stone figures carved by the people of San Agustín. VI century B.C.– A.D. XII century.

stone: the sculptures of San Agustín, the underground burial chambers of the Tierradentro, and the architectural complexes of the Tayrona.

Not far from San Agustín, more stone carvers were working diligently, carving burial chambers into the soft mountain faces to store the ashes of their sacred leaders. The extraordinary, decorated chambers have high vaulting ceilings, held up with massive columns. Among archaeological ruins, the discovery of Ciudad Perdida on a spur of the Sierra Nevada de Santa Marta signified an extremely important step toward broadening our knowledge and understanding of the ancient culture of the Tayrona. Located on a side of Corea Mountain, the city is made up of over one hundred foundations on top of stone terraces, which are interconnected by a central path and several other lateral ones—an early example of the grid system. The principal road starts on the lowest level of the city, on the shores of the Buritaca River, and ascends to the upper terraces, which are supported by thick retaining walls. The Tayrona worked stone in great blocks; with these blocks and slabs they built rings, roads, long and ascending paths, stairs, bridges, systems for gathering water and sewage, as well as for irrigating their fields. The paths were constructed with different kinds of stone—slabs of slate, carved granite, or polished stone—depending on the importance of the section being constructed. The

From left to right: a caryatid in the shape of a warrior; an eagle —or snake hawk—devouring a snake; a female figure with curved fingers; a pilaster in the shape of a warrior. San Agustín, Huila.

Thousands of years ago a civilization developed along the banks of the Magdalena River in what is today Colombia. It was a remarkable culture; its people built massive (over ten feet high) stone figures and carved elaborate

burial chambers beneath the ground. This site was discovered in the middle of the eighteenth century, by which time its inhabitants had long since disappeared. Little is known about the builders of this mysterious place, San Agustín, but it is clear from these monolithic remains that they had complex funerary rites. These monuments are among the most spectacular artifacts left behind by any of the ancient Colombian cultures.

principal pavements at the beginning of the road are of granite and form a perfectly polished, paved surface. In funerary art, the Tayrona used stone to construct their mortuary chambers. The chambers contained rectangular tombs with stone walls and floors and shaft tombs. The sculptural art of these various cultures indicates an impressive evolution of techniques, fueled, in large part, by religious needs.

Smaller scale ceremonial, utilitarian, and ornamental objects were manufactured by the early settlers of Colombia. Stone spoons in the shape of shells were used to serve coca leaves, stone staffs crowned by an eagle or bird of prey were used by religious leaders in rituals, and mortars in the shape of stone tables or ashlars were made for grinding. Many different kinds of stone such as granite, quartz, rock crystal, cornelian, and jadeite provided these first stoneworkers with a broad range of colors for their necklaces, breastplates, and plaques: translucent white, opaque white, red, black, gray, and green. Rock crystal was used to make necklace beads and ritual objects.

During the Colonial period, stone was commonly used for vast buildings, churches, convents, and fortresses. The facades were frequently exquisitely worked stone. In the central plazas, stone was used for fountains. Columns that supported pilasters and arches, so common to this

A pedestal carved with geometric and floral patterns. XVIII century. Hacienda Calibío, Popayán, Cauca.

Opposite. Pre-Columbian tools—such as axe heads and stone cutters—were made from stone as iron was not available.

period, were also made of stone. Many splendid examples of Colonial stone architecture can be found in the cities of Cartagena, Popayán, Tunja, Mompós, and Bogotá.

The walls of Cartagena—particularly those of San Felipe—are a magnificent example of how stone was used throughout the Conquest and Colonial period. The strategic value of the stone walls and forts was more than proven by the Spaniards' defense of the city against innumerable pirate attacks. Stone carving—both as fine art and utilitarian craft—continues today in most regions of Colombia.

But, more important than its ample supply of granite, slate, or quartz, Colombia produces the largest and purest emeralds in the world. These most highly valued of gemstones are found in veins along the eastern chain of the Colombian Andes in streaks, dikes, or fractures of sedimentary rock. The veins are exposed with the help of dynamite, and once located, the emeralds are sprayed with water and extracted with stonecutter's hammers, chisels, and mallets. Although the mines are actually owned by the state, they are often exploited by private enterprises. The most important mines are in Boyacá—Muzo, Coscuez, Chivor, Peñas Blancas—and in Cundinamarca—Bellavista. There are at least ten mines in production today and still many emeralds left in the country, despite

the hordes that left on Spanish ships to return to the Old World. Among the pre-Hispanic Colombian populations, and especially among the Muzo and Chibcha, emeralds were a sign that the earth was sacred and worthy of care and worship—rather than symbols of power and magnificence, as they were to the Spanish. The Indians saw a mythical reflection of divinities in the stones, and they wove curious legends and fantastic tales around the creation of such gems. The Muzo revered emeralds as descendants of protective gods.

The finest emeralds, those that present an intensely green color of exceptional brilliance, are known by the name "drop of oil." These are found only in the Muzo mines of Colombia. The Spanish were astounded when they discovered the source of these spectacular gems and carried them back to Europe by the shipload. The monstrance, known in Colombia as "La Lechuga"—or "The

A stone water channel. XVIII century. Popayán, Cauca.

Opposite. Pre-Columbian pestle and mortar. Similar pieces have been found throughout the country, which makes it probable that corn was widely cultivated in Colombia. Atlántico.

Following pages. Pre-Columbian stone necklaces. These colorful strands of quartz, jade, onyx, and cornelian, interspersed with metal beads, were found in the remains of several ancient settlements. The meticulously cut stones show the splendid stoneworking skills of early Colombians, who wore such necklaces as part of their everyday attire. Various cultures.

Lettuce"—is the most outstanding representative of Colonial ecclesiastical art. Cast in gold between 1700 and 1707, it was embossed, engraved, and adorned with thousands of precious stones. Because of the profuse use of emeralds, estimated to number nearly fifteen hundred separate stones, it is affectionately compared to a head of lettuce. It is supported on a pedestal or column, which rises from a round base and sustains the splendid sunburst that houses the Holy Eucharist. The angel's garments are enameled in emerald and sapphire dust and the red that adorns the boots comes from ground rubies. Encrusted over its surface are pearls, amethysts, rubies, topaz, and diamonds. Colombia's contemporary jewelers continue to set new standards for design using this entrancingly beautiful gemstone.

Between the pure Colombian gold and the finest emeralds in the world, the natural riches of this country are extraordinary.

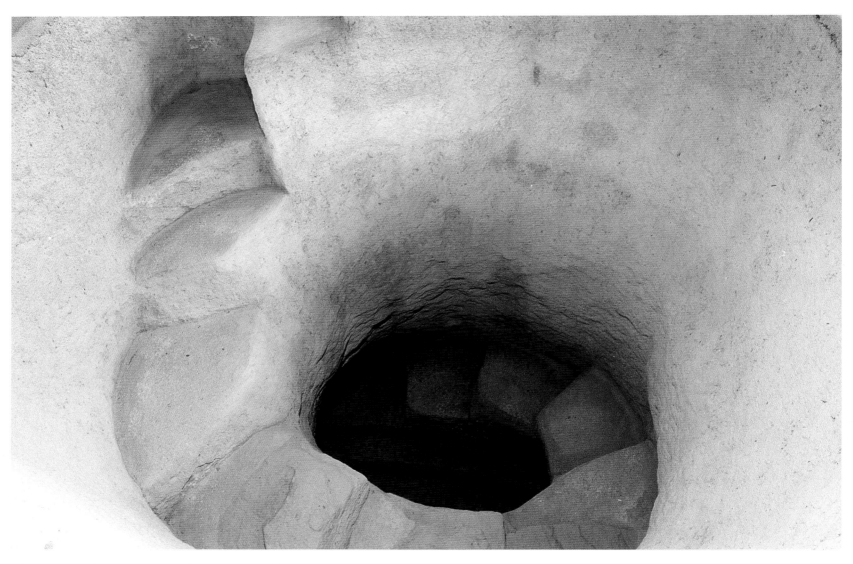

Above. A spiral staircase, carved in rock, leads down to an underground burial chamber. Its entrance was sealed with a heavy stone slab. Around the same time as the San Agustín culture, across the Cordillera Occidental in Tierradentro, another mysterious civilization flourished that was only discovered this century by grave robbers. These people of Tierradentro, which means "within the earth," laboriously carved burial chambers out of the soft rock of the mountainside to hold the ashes of important members of their communities. A.D. VI century. Tierradentro, Cauca.

Opposite. A burial chamber carved into the mountain face. The walls and ceilings of these chambers were decorated with geometric and anthropomorphic shapes. This one held the ashes of seven people. A.D. VI century. Tierradentro, Cauca.

Left. Esplanades and flagstone terraces of the Tayrona culture. The Tayrona, who lived from about the first to the sixteenth century A.D., were superb builders and urban planners. More than 250 of their settlements have been found, entangled in the tropical jungles of the Sierra Nevada de Santa Marta. They constructed elevated terraces along steep mountain slopes, with flagstoned "plazas" around which were built their dwellings. This settlement, Ciudad Perdida—or "the lost city"—is thought to be their capital. The Tayrona scattered and died out not long after the arrival of the Spanish, but the Kogui Indians living in the area today—possibly descendants of the original inhabitants—provide clues to this culture of extraordinary builders.

Right. A stone pathway of Ciudad Perdida. Although this city was only recently discovered, most of it has been cleared from the encroaching jungle and restored. These pathways connected the various mountain terraces, but also served as channels to drain rainwater. The structures that survive today, despite the often precarious siting along steep mountainsides and the torrential rainfalls of the jungle, are a testament to the Tayrona's sophisticated hydraulics. The crucial drainage points were elaborately marked with carved stones and great stone slabs. Offerings for guardian spirits were left under the slabs. Ciudad Perdida, Sierra Nevada de Santa Marta, Magdalena.

Left. Founded by the Spanish in the sixteenth century, Cartagena became a bustling Colonial port on the edge of the Caribbean. Spanish adventurers often stopped here, laden with treasures, before sailing for home; thus it also fell prey to pirate attacks. To protect the city and their goods, the Spanish fortified the port, building enormous stone ramparts that did, indeed, prove impregnable. XVII – XVIII century. Cartagena, Bolívar.

Right. In the savannah on the outskirts of Bogotá lie numerous salt deposits. This underground chapel was carved from a great salt mine cavern earlier in this century. It is reached through long, illuminated tunnels. The deposits of Nemocón, where this church is located, and the nearby town of Zipaquirá have been mined since pre-Columbian times.

Above. The stone bench, plant shed, steps, and ground outside this home indicate the importance of masonry as a Colonial building material in Colombia. Bogotá.

Left. The facade of the Church of San Agustín. XVII century. Bogotá.

Above. A stonemason carving the capital of a column. Bojacá, Cundinamarca.

Right. The doorways of Colonial homes were usually made of adobe and brick; only the entrances to homes of important families—such as this one—were made of stone. The lintel and jambs here are unusually large chunks of quarrystone. Bogotá.

Above. Paving blocks of different quarrystones in the Plaza de Santo Domingo.   XVIII century. Popayán, Cauca.

Above. This stone-and-brick floor of a Colonial home fans out in geometric diagonals from the central fountain of the patio. XVIII century. Bogotá.

Above. Floor made from river stones, clay tiles, and animal vertebrae. XIX century. Bogotá.

Above. The design of this river-stone pavement outside a country home is contemporary, but clearly influenced by traditional techniques. La Pintada, Caldas.

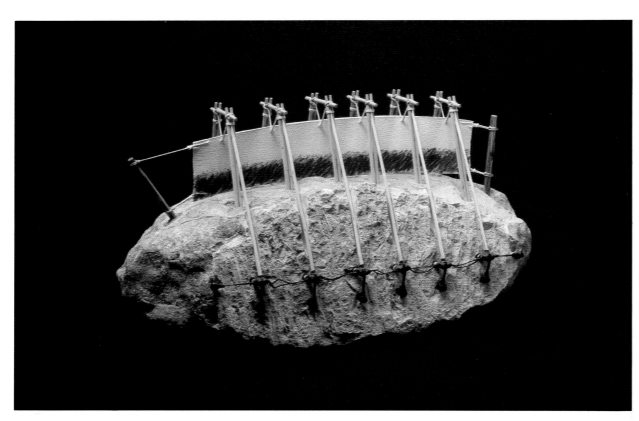

Above. Contemporary sculpture of a boat in stone and wood. Ezequiel Alarcón, Barichara, Santander.

Below. An ashtray, mortar, and bowl carved from the rustic marble of Villa de Leyva. Galería Deimos, Bogotá.

Opposite. Glass table with inlaid stone slabs on two sides. The floor, which is also finely worked stone, is visible through the glass. Hugo Zapata, Medellín, Antioquia.

WEAVING

At first glance there seems to be little in common between a small hat and a hammock, a reed basket and a blanket, but in fact, all are produced by weaving. Weaving methods and techniques are as varied as the materials that are being used. All kinds of pliable fibers found in nature, as well as man-made yarns, can be woven into textiles or objects.

A tropical climate such as Colombia's yields plants of many kinds whose leaves, stems, bark, and roots lend themselves to weaving—either almost as they are grown or after various methods of preparation. Likewise, cotton and hemp have been used from the earliest times for textiles.

Archaeological finds tell us that weaving was well-developed in regions of Colombia, such as Quindío, Cundinamarca, Boyacá, and Santander—long before the arrival of the Spaniards. However, the finds are not as plentiful as in Guatemala or Peru, where the drier climates have helped to preserve fabric intact for centuries. Textiles disintegrate quickly in the damp air and acid soil prevalent in many parts of Colombia.

The chronicles of sixteenth-century travelers in the region describe painted cotton garments from Antioquia and Caldas and finely painted cotton mantles produced by the Chibcha people. These textiles were so highly regarded that given as a gift, they were considered an expression of homage.

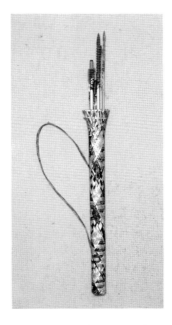

An arrow quiver woven in yarumo palm fiber by the Indians living in the plains of eastern Colombia. Vichada.

Opposite. A mochila — traditional shoulder bag— and hats of the Arhuaco Indians. Sierra Nevada de Santa Marta, Magdalena.

The finest woven artifacts—reserved for special events both by men and women and held in place by golden pins—represented luxury and social standing.

Wool was not known in Colombia until the Conquest when the Spaniards introduced sheep to the area. At first, sheep's wool was carded and spun into yarn with simple tools; the yarn was then woven on primitive vertical looms. Later, the horizontal loom and spinning wheel were introduced. What had once amounted to a very limited, complex production slowly expanded to become a veritable industry, which reached its height in the nineteenth century. In parallel with the mechanization of wool preparation, spinning, and weaving, the old traditions continued largely unchanged. Artisans in many communities still weave on plain vertical or back-strap looms, with yarns deftly twisted by hand and spindle; in remote areas the craft of weaving has scarcely altered over hundreds of years.

Today, the textile tradition is richly represented throughout the country; each region displays its own preferences for materials, colors, styles, and patterns. Cotton is abundantly cultivated in the temperate and hot regions; sheep-rearing is common in the cooler plains, and the silk worm, newly introduced into Colombia, is giving every indication that it will adapt and provide a new raw material for the textile industry. Even in territories such as Antioquia, where the raw materials—cotton and wool—are not so prevalent, the textile industry is considered one of the most prestigious and productive in Latin America. A simple craft has turned itself into a healthy industry.

Pita fiber, or hemp, is undoubtedly one of the most commonly used fibers in all of Colombia. "From the pack saddle on the donkey descending the high barren moors with his baskets full of charcoal," wrote Eduardo Caballero Calderón in his book, *Tipacoque*, "to the girth of the horse on which Bolívar scaled the Andes: breast bands, halters, tethers, lead ropes, shoulder bags, twine, rope-soled sandals, sacks, ropes, a completely *mestizo* culture from the high moors and hot lowlands, for donkeys and horses, for dandies and Indians, is woven with the golden pita fiber." A native American plant, it will tolerate practically all climates and grows profusely, especially in the Colombian Andes.

Many areas produce specialized items for which they have become known far and wide. Along the Caribbean, in the department of Bolívar, one can find weavers making hammocks, shoulder bags, bedspreads, and cushions in a spectacular array of colors that reflect the vivacity of the tropical forest. Their sense of style is highly original and they skillfully mix yarns of vivid and contrasting hues to produce a pleasing and harmonic whole.

Detail of macramé with braided silk fringes. Shawls are part of the traditional clothing of the Andean region, but this silken one is reserved for special occasions. Gachancipá, Cundinamarca.

The *mochila* is a woven shoulder bag that has been used for centuries by the fishermen and farmers of the Caribbean—particularly the Arhuacos, whose magnificent bags are highly sought after. Many versions and shapes of the *mochila* have found their way to other parts of the country. *Mochilas* can be made from a variety of materials such as wool, cotton, and plant fibers. In Atánquez, a small town in northern Colombia, they are most frequently made from hemp that is readily available there near the Sierra Nevada de Santa Marta mountains. *Mochilas* are woven most often by women, and worn—two or three at a time—by both sexes.

In La Guajira, the desert peninsula that juts out from the northernmost part of the country, the tradition of weaving is so deeply rooted that it is said the Guajiro women "weave until is it time for loving." In almost every Guajiro settlement, outdoor vertical looms are visible and on these the weavers (always female in this region) create their *chinchorros*—elaborately decorated hammocks. The Guajiro is born, lives, and dies in his chinchorro and even then he does not part from it; it accompanies him to his grave. The patterns incorporated in the *chinchorro* are traditional and have varied little from generation to generation. A finely woven *chinchorro* has both symbolic value and a real value. In the marketplace, it is worth more than a head of cattle.

Artisans in other areas, such as Nariño, specialize in hand-knotted carpets and in the colder climates, Colombian ponchos—or *ruanas*—and belts are woven in lively colors. The Páez and Guambiano Indians, on the other hand, weave mostly dark blue and gray wool with magenta and black detailing for their shawls and ponchos, following a centuries-old tradition. And the Arhuacos and Koguis weave even plainer ponchos of undyed wool and cotton.

Mantles and blankets are produced in the craft centers of Pasto, Ipiales, Puerres,Túquerres, Gualtamán, and other smaller towns. In Boyacá, one can find the largest flocks of sheep.The department's most important textile centers produce soft woolen flannels, as well as thick baize mostly used for ponchos, mantles, and shoulder bags.

In the eighteenth century, in the department of Valle, a small factory was opened to stimulate production using pita fiber. Until recently, small factories there and in Antioquia and Boyacá were able to meet the country's demands for pita products. But with the gradual industrialization of Colombia, larger-scale factories were established to supply the needs of a growing market. On the crafts level, pita is turned into belts, bags, hammocks, carpets, place mats, and perhaps most importantly, *alpargatas*. The *alpargata* is a sandal-type shoe first introduced by the Spaniards. It has

Cloth figurines from a nativity crèche. Popayán, Cauca.

Contemporary basketry of straw and dyed pita fibers. Saboyá, Boyacá.

braided hemp soles and woven-cotton uppers and heel straps. *Alpargatas* are worn throughout rural Colombia; their decorations, often in black thread vary somewhat from region to region.

The Caribbean Indians of Chocó stitch together "patch-work like" tapestries—or *molas*—whose lively colors echo the brilliance of the coastal waters and exotic flora of the region. *Molas* are made with several layers of woven cloth. A figure or pattern is cut out of one layer, and the remaining fabric is carefully hemmed and stitched to the background cloth. This process is repeated, each time exposing a different layer of the cloth beneath it. The Cuna people create splendid tapestries with depth of color and intricate designs. Originally made as decorative panels to adorn women's blouses, *molas* now fetch high prices as wall hangings. The smaller the stitches, the higher the value of the piece.

Basketry is a free form of weaving that requires no other equipment than the material itself. It can therefore be done anywhere that reeds, roots, long grasses, pliable twigs, and other fibers can be found. It is one of the earliest crafts to develop in primitive societies; it probably preceded even pottery, which then evolved naturally from it. One can imagine a nomadic people traveling through an area rich in edible plants and fruits, stopping to make baskets in order to carry more food along.

Colombian basketry today comprises a variety of techniques and designs, which are the result of strong, well-developed traditions that have endured and evolved to incorporate new shapes and forms compatible with contemporary needs. In the Vaupés jungle, the basketry is particularly fine. The artisan's staple material is a fiber derived from the *yarumo* palm, which grows abundantly in the area. In addition, he gathers hemp and makes tar and vegetable dyes. He colors the fibers to be used as the weft of his baskets and leaves the warp plain. In Vaupés, basketry is a man's craft. All kinds of objects for household use are made by weaving together plant fibers. In addition to baskets for carrying food, they produce colanders, sifters used for preparing cassava dough, flexible cylindrical juicers to extract poisonous juices from cassava, and a fan that can be used to enliven a cooking fire or flip over cassava cakes. The shapes of the baskets have evolved over the years to better suit their maker's needs; the Indians who live along the Vaupés River have devised a clever basket form whose convex bottom allows it to sit on the floor of a canoe without getting wet.

The banks along the Amazon and Orinoco rivers are rife with fibrous plants, which the Indians use for their basketry: palm fronds, tree barks, and *chocolatillo*, a small fibrous plant. These soft fibers are ideal for making loosely woven hammocks and bags, as well as a variety of

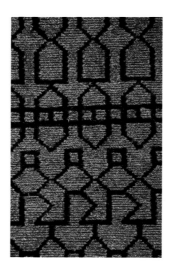

A horsehair tapestry. Olga de Amaral, Bogotá.

Opposite. The roof of a communal house in woven palm fibers. Rió Mirití, Caquetá.

baskets. Symmetrical, geometric patterns are typical of baskets from this region.

Along the Pacific Coast, as well, indigenous communities produce trunks and banana baskets out of *chocolatillo* fiber, which they first tint with a vegetable dye. In a combination of black and brown, the baskets—especially those from Cauca in southern Colombia, feature characteristics borrowed from African cultures that distinguish them from other indigenous basketry.

The Emberá people who live in the jungles along the Pacific, in an area where palms and reeds grow abundantly, make much of the objects and equipment they need for everyday life out of these raw materials. They start weaving at an early age and almost all the items they produce are used within the community, not with an eye for trade. They sleep upon woven mats, transport food packed in hemp, and store possessions in woven baskets. They also make hats and fishing nets from palm fibers. In addition, they weave toys in the shapes of familiar animals, such as crabs.

Artisans among the Noanamá use fibers of *güerregue*, a jungle palm, to make baskets of great beauty. These master basket weavers have a varied ornamental repertory and have developed an almost unbelievable technique that allows them to intertwine plant fibers so precisely and tightly that the resulting baskets can hold liquids. With their magnificent and varied geometric

designs, they possess an abstract beauty and are among the most sought after and admired of Colombian artifacts.

In rural Colombia, the forms of basketry definitely follow function. In the Cordilleras, the mountains that form part of the Andes, the temperate climate and topography are ideal for coffee growing. Antioquia and Caldas are the richest coffee-growing regions in the country. There, and in the department of Huila, one can find "coffee baskets" for use at harvest time, as well as for washing and storing coffee beans.

The resourceful Colombian artisan will work with whatever material is available. In some parts of the country, where the appropriate plant fibers are not accessible, ropes, girths for saddles, and even saddlebags can be woven or braided from horsehair. The rural areas to the south of the Tota Lagoon are known for their horsehair nets and strainers. The giant reeds that grow in this region are also put to use and woven together into animal cages, flutes, and imaginative toys.

The Usiacurí people in the department of Atlántico continue a tradition of delicate, lace-like basketry. By using metal wire for the framework of their baskets they can make them durable in spite of the lightness of their weave. The wire is covered with a straw fiber so that the waste baskets, decanter covers, coffe, and bread baskets produced in this way have a natural finish.

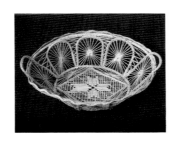

A bread basket in iraca palm *fiber. Usiacurí, Atlántico.*

Woman wearing a traditional straw hat. Puerto Estrella, Guajira.

Opposite. A sieve in yarumo *fiber for sifting cassava. Vaupés.*

The making of straw hats—based on the same techniques as basketry—is a craft practiced all across the country. More than one hundred types of hats can be found, demonstrating the many ingenious solutions artisans have devised for covering and adorning their heads.

The use of hats in Colombia dates back to pre-Hispanic times. The country's earliest inhabitants—particularly those along the Caribbean—protected themselves from the relentless sun. The Spaniards introduced not only new hat styles, but laws concerning their manufacture and use to denote economic standing.

In the interior, on the high plains of Boyacá, the *tapia pisada* or *adobe* hat is still being manufactured. The origins of its design can be traced back to the Spanish *córdoba*, though there has been visible native intervention. Variations of this hat are made across the country and are called the Palmeado, Rancher, High Crown, Common, and Cowboy hat, to name a few.

The product of the master Nariño hat maker became an important export item in the early 1900s, when it caught on as a warm-weather head cover across the United States. The craft became most highly developed in Huila in the town of Sauza, where the women dedicated themselves to hat making. These Sauza—or Panama—hats achieved world renown.

The wide-brimmed *corrosca* is an integral part of the dress and personality of the cow-punching plains' men of the Llanos Orientales. Light-weight and light-colored, it shields the *llanero*, who is usually in the saddle from sunrise to sundown, from the fierce sun.

Enormously popular both at home and abroad, the flat brimmed *vueltiao* is native to the Sinú region. Its geometric designs, intricately woven in black and white strands of arrow reed, form totemic symbols that are thought to have their roots in the Maya culture. Excavated ceramic and gold pieces show pictures and shapes with the same designs. Years ago, family clans could be identified by the decorations woven in their hats. This sense of artistic belonging has vanished over time so that now, only the least complicated and most familiar patterns have survived among the *vueltiao* hat makers. Recently, the same black and

Detail of a traditional woolen horsecloth. Nobsa, Boyacá.

Beaded Indian ornaments. Noanamá Indians, Chocó.

white patterns have also found their way into bags and other woven items.

The making of straw hats, deeply rooted in many rural communities, was transformed by the introduction of the wool or felt hat. It quickly became popular among the farming population, especially in higher, colder areas and reduced the domestic demand for straw hats. Even so, the great variety of raw materials and styles still being made places Colombia ahead of most other hat-making nations.

The weavers of Colombia continue to work today in what is perhaps the oldest craft tradition known to mankind; they are ingenious artisans whose baskets, hats, bags, ponchos, and hammocks have met utilitarian needs while expanding aesthetic boundaries. The fact that many of their creations can now be bought around the world is a testament to their enormous skill.

Opposite. Detail of the embroidery of a chasuble woven in silver, gold, and silk threads. This elaborate technique is reserved for ecclesiastical vestments. XVIII century. Popayán, Cauca.

Opposite. Pre-Columbian ceramic whorls with incised decoration. The whorl, used in weaving, is the bottom part of the spindle. It is pierced by a small cane with a hook at one end, so that when the spinner makes it rotate freely, its movement twists the fibers passing through it. Different cultures.

Right.
Top. Most early woven artifacts have not survived the humid Colombian climate; but a few pre-Columbian fragments still exist to show us the methods of the country's first weavers. This fabric was woven in twisted cotton and colored with vegetable dyes. Muisca culture.

Bottom left. This shawl fragment was woven on an early loom. Dyed threads were distributed in the warp according to color to achieve the geometric patterns. A.D. XI–XV century. Guane culture.

Below right. Fragment of pre-Columbian cotton fabric, painted with vegetable dyes. Muisca culture.

Following pages. Chinchorros hung out at a Wayuu settlement. The hammocks of these nomadic desert dwellers are highly prized and considered symbols of prestige. They are custom-woven to accommodate the exact size of the user and are not slept in lengthwise, but with the head and feet along the short sides.

Above. Details of warp and fabric
of a hammock woven in cotton on
a vertical loom. San Jacinto,
Bolívar.

Left. Cotton chinchorros—or
hammocks—for sale. San Onofre,
Sucre.

Opposite. Chinchorro *in cumare
palm fiber. This type is made by
interlacing thin, long cords
horizontally around two vertical
posts. The transverse lengths are
placed in pairs and interwoven
alternately with two longitudinal
threads, until they number four
hundred. Llanos Orientales.*

Opposite and above. Chinchorros of the Guajira woven in brilliantly colored cotton thread. The Wayuu make two kinds of chinchorros: those based on warp weaving and those with a single chain-stitch or a double chain-stitch for the weft, which is generally double-sided. Elaborate flounces are stitched to the edges of the hammocks. Wayuu Indians, Guajira.

Left. Mochilas woven in pita fiber. Atlántico.

Right. Pérsides Criollo finishes weaving the base of a pita fiber mochila. Sandoná, Nariño.

Mochilas—or traditional shoulder bags—have been a part of everday dress in Colombia for centuries. They are worn over the shoulders or attached to sashes around the waist. Often one person will carry several at a time, strapped around either arm. They are usually made by a female weaver, who begins with a small crocheted disk, in either cotton, wool, or vegetable fibers, which is then built up with a perforated blunt needle into a circular base. The sides of the bag are then stitched from the edge of this base in brightly colored, contrasting fibers. The upper border is finished with a double row of tassles. The introduction of the crochet hook by Spanish missionaries sometime in the seventeenth century brought about a splendid explosion of designs.

Opposite. Guambiano Indian women, from the stephills of the Andes. One of them is starting to weave a mochila in pita fiber, while another winds wool she has spun. The women wear a series of anacos or loose skirts of blackish wool, decorated with horizontal, colored bands, which the women themselves weave on a vertical loom. The skirts are tied at the waist with a bright sash or chumbe. Around their shoulders the women wrap at least four blue shawls, which are held together with metal pins. Silvia, Cauca.

Above. Alejo Agreda, Kamsha Chief, weaving a net. He wears a characteristic poncho. The Kamsha Indians, who live high in the Andes, number about 4,000 today. They live by farming and the sale of their crafts. San Francisco, Putumayo.

Right. A Guajira mochila *woven in cotton. Makú, Guajira.*

Opposite. Mochilas *made in the Guajira, a semi-arid peninsula in the northernmost part of the country, are woven only from colorful cotton threads. Elsewhere, other natural fibers are used. The* mochilas *from this region can be recognized by their particularly lively and complex designs. The* talegas, *as they are also known, are made in various shapes and sizes to carry anything from small change to hammocks and heavy objects. At the lower right are bags from Sierra Nevada de Santa Marta. The colors of* mochilas *from this mountainous region are less brilliant; white* mochilas *are worn by the spiritual leaders— or Mamas—of the Kogui Indians who live here.*

Following pages. Sashes—or siíras—*woven in cotton threads.* Siíras, *which are worn to hold up* guayucos—*or loincloths—are made with brightly colored threads and finished with long fringes and tassles. Wayuu Indians, Guajira.*

130

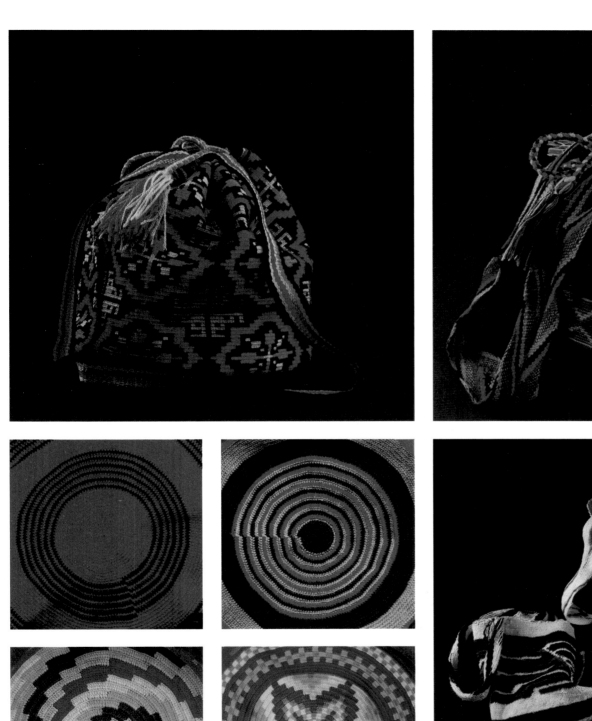
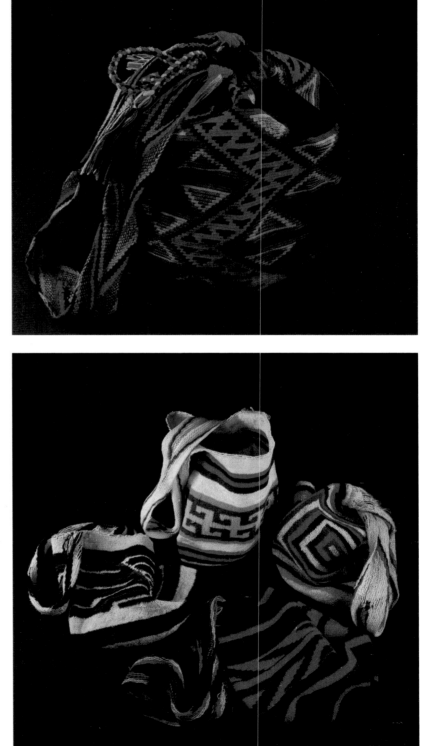

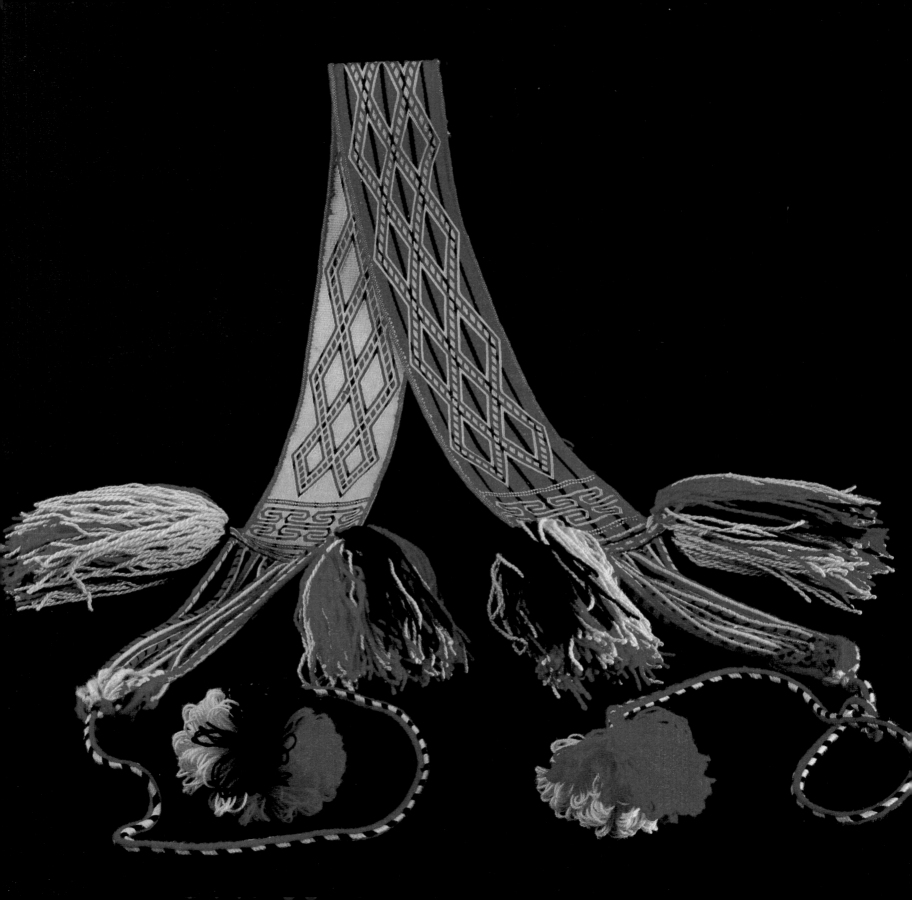

Above left. Blankets in natural-colored wool with colored stripes, made in sack and herringbone stitches. This small Colonial town of Villa de Leyva has attracted a number of artisans over the years, particularly weavers. Every weekend, townspeople gather in the Plaza de Mayor to buy and sell their wares, including these fine blankets. Villa de Leyva, Boyacá.

Above right. Blanket woven on a horizontal loom with different fibers of dyed wool over a died cotton warp. Ricardo Carrizosa, Tabio, Cundinamarca.

Below. Horsecloth made on a loom in tufted wool on spun cotton. These small, knotted blankets were traditionally placed under the saddle of a horse. Today, they are used as wall ornaments or bedside rugs. Nobsa, Boyacá.

Opposite. Woman weaving woolen fabric for a poncho on a vertical loom. In rural areas, looms are seen outside nearly every home. Santa Rosa, Santander.

Opposite.

Top left. Open ruana—*or* poncho— *in virgin wool made on a horizontal loom. Ricardo Carrizosa, Tabio, Cundinamarca.*

Top right. Young soccer fans dressed in woolen ruanas. *Boyacá.*

Bottom. Classical ruanas *woven in virgin wool on a vertical loom and then brushed to raise the nap. Sogamoso, Boyacá.*

Left. Details of ruanas. *Two separate pieces are joined together, leaving an opening for the head. Cundinamarca and Boyacá.*

Paired with straw hats, ruanas *are the characteristic dress of Colombians who live in the colder climates, thousands of feet high up in the Andes. The ponchos are made in two pieces, generally of natural-colored white, gray, or brown wool and each piece measures approximately twenty-five by fifty-five inches. They are woven on a four-pole loom and the warp is always thinner and finer than the weft. When weaving is complete, the pieces are stitched together by hand, and the cloth is then brushed. Ruanas are also woven with designs of stripes or squares.*

Above. Brightly colored alpargatas—or sandals—woven in cotton, with pita fiber soles. Chiquinquirá, Boyacá.

Top left. Alpargatas and molds for weaving the toecaps. The sole is traditionally of braided pita fiber and the toecap is of cotton. Monguí, Boyacá.

Bottom left. Sandals woven in dyed vegetable fibers with a sole of rubber or leather. Makú, Guajira.

Opposite. Sandals woven in wool with an embossed leather sole. These are traditionally worn by the women of the dry Guajira peninsula. They are formed by braided woolen cords fixed to a leather sole with three holes. The tops are decorated with woolen tassels, which vary in size in accordance with the social standing of the wearer. Makú, Guajira.

Left. "Patchwork" piece made of cut fabric. Cuna Indians, Golfo de Urabá, Chocó.

These fabric squares—or molas—are made by the Cuna Indians who live in the rain forest along the Panamanian border. Today, they are most often hung upon walls, but originally, they were attached by Cuna women to the fronts and backs of their blouses. The process is a very meticulous one—the artisan begins by stacking several squares of differently colored fabric on top of each other. She then cuts a pattern into the stack, revealing just one of the underlayers. This pattern is hemmed down—and the fabric squares secured together—by minute stitches. The process is then repeated to expose a different underlayer. The value of the mola is determined by the number of layers and the size of the stitches. Each piece takes between one and three weeks to complete.

*Above. Wall hanging made from
a number of "patchwork" squares
of the Cuna Indians with stylized
animal figures, stitched together.
Clara Lucía de Villegas, Bogotá.*

Opposite.
Top. A roof being constructed with bitter palm branches, placed over and tied with reeds to a wooden structure. Amazonas.

Bottom left. Panniers with a slanted weft in yarumo fiber, braided in a spiral from the base. These baskets can be made quickly and are used to store, preserve, and transport cassava flour. Amazonas.

Bottom center and right. Catarijanos—Indian baskets made by braiding the leaves and veins of palm branches. They are used throughout the rain forest to collect and transport fruit and foodstuffs. Every inhabitant of the Amazon learns as a child how to make such baskets quickly, from whatever leaves are available. Río Cahuinarí, Amazonas.

Right. Roof of a school hut of coconut palm branches, tied with reeds over a conical, wooden structure. Sierra de la Macuira, Guajira.

Opposite. Mats woven in palm fiber on a string warp. Green palm leaves, shredded and hung to dry and whiten in the sun, are used for these mats. They were traditionally dyed with annatto and are used as floor coverings. Ovejas, Sucre.

Top right. Agricultural products are wrapped in these plantain bark mats to facilitate transportation. In the background are rush mats. Barbosa, Santander.

Bottom right. Rush mats for sale. They are used as mattresses or to protect horses, mules, and donkeys from the loads they carry. The rushes grow in abundance in marshy areas in cold or temperate climates. Tota, Boyacá.

Opposite. Horsehair sieves woven on a rustic loom. The loom is built with three poles and three additional rods that cross the warp perpendicularly to bring all the threads together. These are knotted into bunches of eight threads, and fixed to the edges with string. The weft is held in place by a small, flat strip of hard wood. The wood is cut and split into sheets that are curved to hold the fabric between the two circles. The fabric thus remains taut and firm and is used to sift a variety of foodstuffs. Tenza, Boyacá.

Above. Detail of a horsehair cinch used to hold the saddle on the back of a horse or donkey. Tota, Boyacá.

Left. Horsehair cords on a vertical loom with warp of the same material. Braided or woven horsehair is extremely strong. Bridle bands and saddle pads are also made with it. Tabio, Cundinamarca.

Following pages. Baskets woven from güerregue palm fiber. The weave is so fine and tight that they can carry liquids. Noanamá Indians, Chocó.

Opposite. Yarumo fiber baskets dyed with tree sap. The unusual shape of the baskets allows them to fit tightly into the prow of a canoe and remain dry. Vaupés.

Above. Plantain bark baskets. The bark is removed from the trunk when it is still green, and then scraped, peeled, and dried in the sun. Manizales, Caldas.

Below. A fiber basket used by women to carry bitter cassava, which is then used to make bread, the staple of the Amazon. Vaupés.

Basketry from the jungles of Vaupés is always woven by men; it is based on palm fibers. The Indians use machetes and knives to cut down and scrape the fibers. The fibers are then manipulated, either by mouth or foot, depending on their role in the basket. The weft is either perpendicular (right) or diagonal (left).

Top. A sebucán—or flexible cassava press—squeezes the poisonous acids out of the cassava root pulp. Puerto Inírida, Guainía.

Bottom. Palm fiber basket for carrying food. The technique behind this is quite straight-forward. After cutting and scraping the fiber, the basket-maker cuts it into long strips. The thickest ones are used for the structure (warp) and the rest for the weft. The first strip is then interlaced over and under the weft to form the base. Following this, the fibers (forming the base) are bent upwards and on this the rest is woven with more flexible, previously treated fibers, until the border is reached. This is finished by doubling the surplus segments back into the structure of the weaving, over reeds rolled spirally into strips to give greater consistency. Vaupés.

Opposite. Details of fiber baskets made by Indians of the Amazon and the Llanos Orientales. The way in which the fiber is woven and dyed, as well as the finishing of the borders, distinguish one group from another. They are used in preparing cassava, a plant with a fleshy root that yields a nutritious starch but must first be processed to extract its poisonous acids. The root is grated and then its pulp is pressed through a sieve-like basket. The siefted pulp is then introduced into a sebucán, shown opposite, and squeezed to draw out the poisonous prussic acid. Since its composition is highly volatile, the acid must be collected in a container with ashes. Here the acid is neutralized and can then be used as a dye. When the purified pulp has dried, it is removed from the press and sifted again through a larger basket. The resulting product is a white, floury powder, which may be used either as cassava or tapioca.

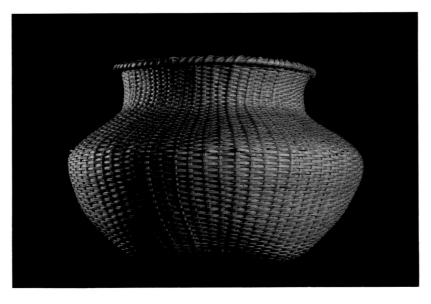

Opposite. Nieves Pinilla weaving hats from thin, rolled braids of palm fiber. They are known as Straw and Clay hats because of their strong, compact weave, which is similar to clay and straw walls. Villa de Leyva, Boyacá.

Top. Hats being aired in the street. This is a traditional practice and is repeated several times with each hat. Sandoná, Nariño.

Bottom. Artisans weaving palm hats. The still unopened palm heart is split vertically and used to make the hats. At the end of the last century, when Panama was still part of Gran Colombia, they were known as Panama hats. Sandoná, Nariño.

155

Above. The Kwari hat of the Guambiano Indian is made of vegetable-dyed cane fiber. It is generally woven by a groom for his bride as a wedding gift, and is from then on worn only during religious ceremonies. Silvia, Cauca.

Below. The "Panama hat" is woven at home by rural and urban families in the country's coffee-growing regions. They are always worn by men while harvesting coffee to protect them from the relentless sun. Aguadas, Caldas.

One artisan begins the hat by making the crown, interlacing dampened palm fibers. She then gives it to another who makes the brim. Once the form is completed, the hat is gummed, aired, soaked in cold water, and then placed on a hat block. Here it is curved by hand and the fold made in the crown. In the final step the hat is polished to give it its white luster.

Right. These black and white hats are worn by the peasants of Córdoba, Sucre, and Bolívar from childhood on. They are named for their many patterned rows—or vueltas. The vueltiao is always made the same way: seven rows of black and white fibers for the top, a black strip edging onto the white strip around the crown, the crown itself of five rows, and twelve rows in the brim, which is finished by a black braid. San Andrés de Sotavento, Córdoba.

WOOD

Nearly half of Colombia is covered in forest; it is not surprising, therefore, to find wood among the raw materials used most often by local artisans over the centuries. Palms, laurel, *guaiacum*, mangrove, mahogany, and cedar trees all grow in the jungles of the Amazon, along the Orinoco River, and by the Pacific Coast. In the Andean highlands, which occupy about one third of the country's land, there are bamboo, giant reeds, walnuts, and many other types of trees. Colombian artisans continue to transform these woods into shelters, canoes, household wares, and furniture—as their ancestors did centuries ago.

While wood was widely used by pre-Columbian builders in construction, there are practically no traces of such structures today. Wood is very sensitive to changes in temperature and has not been able to withstand the humidity of the Colombian climate. It is also, of course, susceptible to fires. We only know of its use in ancient buildings from miniature clay models that have survived and show wood as a support structure for buildings and through chronicles from the Conquest, which confirm the presence of wooden products among most pre-Columbian cultures. *Malocas and tambos,* traditional wooden and thatched dwellings, are still built today by indigenous people and can be seen as a perpetuation of an ancient tradition.

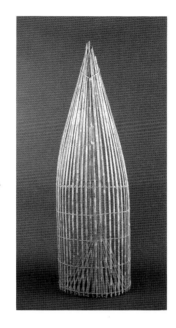

Tucuma *palm fibers strapped together with reeds to form a fishing basket. Miriti-Paraná, Amazonas.*

Opposite. Carved wood sacrarium resplendently gilded with gold leaf. The hinge is cast in silver and embossed. XVIII century. Popayán, Cauca.

As a result of the Spanish conquest, South Americans came into contact with new ways to transform nature, as practiced by the cabinetmakers of Europe. During the sixteenth and seventeenth centuries, woodworkers from Spain settled in Quito, not far from the current Colombian border, importing the Mudéjar—or Spanish-Moorish—and Flemish styles of architecture to the workshops of the New World. The newly learned skills traveled north and were combined with traditional ones to create a synthesized new style that is still seen today in Colombia.

During the Colonial era, a woodworking industry flourished. The Church was a primary client, commissioning architectural detailwork and statuary to enliven chapels and church interiors. The figures of saints were usually worked in precious hardwoods, which could be found in almost all parts of the country. After carving, the statues were carefully painted so that the sacred images would project a high degree of realism and emotion. Modeled initially, of course, on styles and tastes of Europe, ecclesiastical art underwent subtle modifications upon reaching the New World. Although iconographic motifs remained unchanged, they received stylistic influences that appear throughout the development of Colonial art—slightly richer coloring, a looser carving style, and in Santafé de Bogotá, the artisans went so far as to apply the physical characteristics of their own people to the faces of saints or figures in nativity scenes. Bogotá, Tunja, Popayán, and Pasto were the most important woodcarving centers in the seventeenth and eighteenth centuries. From their workshops came the finest carvings.

Thonet—or bentwood—furniture, named after the German furniture designer, Michael Thonet, arrived in Colombia in the latter part of the nineteenth century. This celebrated technical innovation was based on the use of heat and water to force strips of wood to curve into desired forms. Thonet's invention required no additional ornamentation or carving to create elegant furniture. The models of the German designer quickly flooded the world's furniture markets. Their simple elegance and comfort proved highly popular in Colombia and cabinetmakers and artisans soon applied the new techniques to a range of regional furnishing needs. Wealthy families commissioned Thonet-style chairs to rock upon their new lattice-worked balconies or to decorate their salons with high, carved wood ceilings. Contemporary furnituremakers and woodworkers continue to innovate in the field, carving delicate architectural flourishes on building interiors and exteriors and creating splendid furniture—mahogany bureaus; and household utensils—lacquered bowls and servers of exotic woods.

Seats carved from a single block of wood by the Indians of the Amazon.

The Indians of the Pacific Coast, the Emberá and Noanamá, carve richly detailed ceremonial staffs from the *meme* or *mare* palm tree. The staffs are used by tribal shamans or medicine men. The figures crowning these staffs are usually naked men or women, but arrows, monkeys, or mating animals are occasionally substituted. Wood plays an important role in the spiritual life of certain Colombian communities; the act of carving wood is considered a sacred one. An apprentice to a shaman begins his training by carving ships out of balsa wood. Only when he has greater dexterity is he allowed to make figures symbolizing spirits or commemorating ancestors. Human figures or wild animal totems are carved in softwoods for children and hardwoods for adults. These coastal Indians also make toys from wood, particularly miniature sailboats—an important plaything for children of the Emberá and Noanamá, many of whom will eventually earn a livelihood from the sea.

In addition to ceremonial objects, the Indians of the Amazon, Vaupés, and Caquetá jungles manufacture wooden articles that are crucial to their survival. They hollow out single trees into canoes for transport along their vital waterways (outboard motors are new, though rather incongruous additions to these ancient forms). And, with remarkable precision they hollow out smaller pieces of wood into blowpipes, bend slender branches into bows, and carve hard twigs into arrows for hunting. Every tribe has its own version of hunting and fishing implements and wind and percussion instruments: cane flutes, calabash maracas, and a great variety of drums. Tree bark is converted, after rigorous treatment, into ceremonial clothing and canvases for painting. The images reproduced in these strange bark paintings are based on the artist's visions while under the influence of *yajé,* a hallucinogenic drug derived from a jungle plant that is ritualistically consumed during ceremonies.

The Sibundoy of Putumayo carve charming scenes of everyday activities, religious images, and masks from the woods found in the southwestern part of the country. Masks play an important, transformative role in the ceremonies of many of Colombia's aboriginal people. Once they are put on, they have the power to transform the human wearers into the gods or mythical beings portrayed on the masks. Since pre-Columbian times, the Tayrona and now their descendants, the Kogui, who inhabit the territory north of the Sierra Nevada de Santa Marta, have incorporated masks into their fertility cults, which revolve around a goddess-figure—the Universal Mother. Masked Kogui dancers perform in rites involving fertilization and cultivation of their fields. In the jungles of the Amazon, masks are associated with the rituals of different groups: the Cubeo carve wooden masks for their funerary rites; the Makuna

Contemporary, ingeniously hinged folding seats in wood. Sabana de Bogotá.

for harvest celebrations; the Yacuna for fertility rites; and the Ticuna wear masks in ceremonies involving rites of passage. Masks and wooden figures are worn and carried during carnival celebrations in Pasto, Riosucio, and Barranquilla; their meanings are strongly rooted in the regional traditions of these people.

The Colombians who live along the Caribbean have a particularly strong wood culture; their homes are usually made from wood, as are the contents of these homes—furniture and household utensils. Since many of these people are fishermen, their livelihood is dependent on their wooden canoes. Artisans also manufacture a variety of articles that are always in demand in the marketplace: basins, spoons, beaters, hammers, cutting boards for the kitchen, and from the sapodilla tree, a large bush that has a soft, reddish wood, they produce forks, beaters, and rolling pins.

Many of the Black communities in Colombia have preserved the woodcarving and sculpting techniques of their African ancestors, although the original meanings of some of the sculptural forms have been lost over the centuries. The wooden basin is used for numerous household chores—for cooking, carrying and washing, as well as for gold panning in rivers. A basin of the same shape serves as a crib for newborn babies, but these versions are richly ornamented.

The artisans of Nariño are known for producing

fine wooden articles for domestic use in their workshops, such as trunks, *bargueños*, boxes, and coffers—plus other lesser handicrafts. The people of Boyacá stand out for their production of musical instruments, as well as other items common to almost every culture: spoons, basins, flatware, cups, glasses, and trays. The majority of their production comes from cottage industries in towns like Chiquinquirá, Socha, Belén, and in the outlying areas near Paipa and Duitama. These are truly artisan towns, populated by industrious people dedicated to the various arts inherited from their ancestors.

But, it is in Chiquinquirá where the region's most prestigious woodworkers are to be found. Stringed musical instruments, guitars, mandolins, treble guitars, and *requintos*—ten-stringed guitars, are produced there with special mastery by dedicated artisans. The fine quality of these instruments is the result of years—centuries—of experience. They are known in the musical world for the delicate clearness of their sound and in the craft world, for their beautiful finish and decoration.

Guadua, a member of the bamboo family, grows wild, abundantly, in the coffee-growing regions of the country—that is, primarily, in Antioquia, Caldas, and Quindío. This fibrous wood, called *bambusa guadua*, is particularly strong and flexible and has played a determining

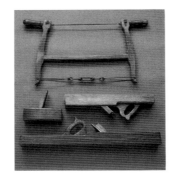

*Saws in a carpenter's workshop.
Manizales, Caldas.*

Opposite. A wardrobe or closet in comino crespo—*a fine wood with zigzagged markings. XIX century. Medellín, Antioquia.*

*Following pages.
Page 164. A rudimentary chair cleverly assembled from four pieces of machete-hewn wood. Guambía, Cauca.*

Page 165. Nearly every male Indian in Colombia carves himself such a stool to use daily while working, chewing coca leaves, chatting, or eating meals. Vaupés.

role in the progress of rural Colombia. In the countryside, *guadua* is a primary building material, instrumental in the development of towns and villages. It provides the structure for houses and the raw material for walls. The roof and ceiling, doors and windows of buildings are also often made of *guadua*. As a gutter or chute to bring water from a nearby stream to the house, or to build a bridge over that same river or stream, *guadua* has proven the ideal engineer's tool. In the kitchen it has become a receptacle for storing grains, honey, and sugar. It is, however, no recent discovery and was used for centuries by pre-Columbian cultures. The Spanish Conquistadors were introduced to *guadua* by the Indians, and imitating their inventions, the Spaniards devised hundreds of new uses for construction and the home. For over five hundred years, the mixture of cultures, Indian and European, have promoted the tradition of *guadua*.

Colombia's wealth and variety of woods continue to be used in all regions to meet the needs of everyday living. Both in rural and urban areas, artisans who intimately know the various properties of all the wood types, obtain the most efficient results from each species, from finely wrought carving and utensils to objects with modern designs that have intrigued the most demanding tastes and markets.

Top. Thonet-style rocking chairs in wood curved by a process using water vapor, with wickerwork back and seat. Developed in Germany in the nineteenth century, this style of furniture has become a standard of Colombia. Caldas.

Bottom left. This is a local version of the Thonet style. Caldas.

Bottom right. Double chair made from mangrove tree roots. Guajira.

Opposite. Table and chair set typically seen in the cafés of the coffee-growing region. Chinchiná, Caldas.

Following pages:
Page 168. Left. Maroon-colored hatrack in cedar wood. John Oberlaender, Bogotá.

Center. A high, elegant table with folding top and walnut wood inlays. John Oberlaender, Bogotá.

Right. A whimsically shaped filing cabinet with mahogany drawers. John Oberlaender, Bogotá.

Page 169. Mahogany table with plywood legs. Santiago Cárdenas, Galería Deimos, Bogotá.

Pages 170–171. Wooden fishing boats made and used daily by the people of Taganga, Magdalena.

Opposite. Walking sticks are used by rural Colombians of all ages. Atlántico.

Right. Ceremonial sticks used by shamans to establish links with the supernatural world. The Noanamá and Emberá live along the Pacific coast in small, traditional communities; the shamans play integral roles in these societies. Noanamá and Emberá Indians, Chocó.

Following pages.
Page 174, left. A set of lances on cane shafts; the tips are carved from hardwood and attached to the shafts with plant fiber. They are used for fishing or hunting small game. Amazonas.

Page 174, right. Blowpipes (details shown) are hollowed out and fitted with poison darts. Although their enormous size (six to eight feet high) make them seem unwieldy, they are actually quite effective for hunting game in the jungle as, unlike the arrow, they make almost no sound when shot. Amazonas.

Page 175. Basketholder made from palm wood, tied with reeds. The shape resembles that of an hourglass and is a symbol of fertility. Amazonas.

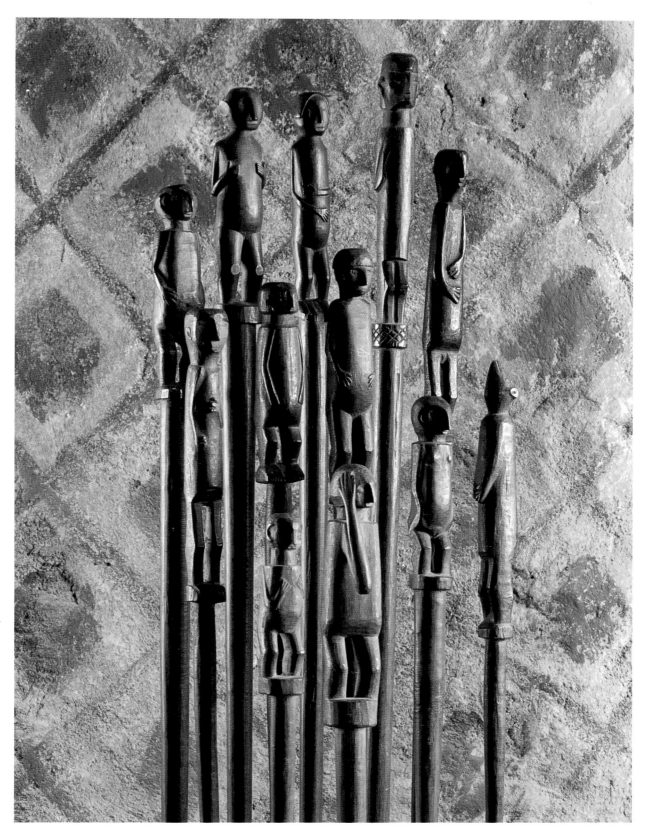

174

Details of bark paintings. The Indians of eastern Colombia remove the inner layer of bark from certain trees and, after initial preparation, paint upon it, as a canvas, with vegetable dyes. Most of the patterns are geometrical, but they often represent animate objects. The triangle, for example, signifies a butterfly, curved lines are snakes, stripes are fish, and squares are parrots. Occasionally, stylized human figures are also incorporated. Bark paintings are found among traditional cultures around the world—including Africa and the South Seas— and are used to make masks and costumes for rituals; they are also highly prized as ornaments. Vaupés and Amazonas.

Masks made from the pith and bark of trees. They are all from different parts of Colombia; most are made by Indians. Top: Sibundoy, Putumayo; bottom left: Macuna, Amazonas; bottom right: Ticuna, Amazonas; opposite page, top left: Torito del Carnaval, Barranquilla; top right: Bogotá; bottom: Macuna, Amazonas.

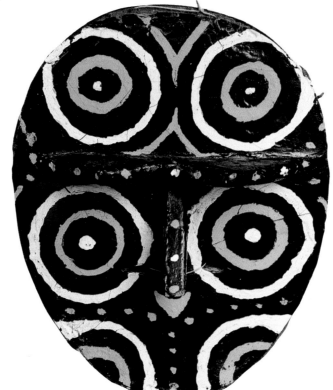

The ritual and ceremonial use of masks among Indian communities began centuries ago and is still a flourishing tradition today. The masks represent spirits—of animals, ancestors, natural forces—that are personified through the wearer. The masked dancer performs during ceremonies to ward off evil, sickness, and death and invoke the spirits of health and goodness.

Masks also play a significant, though less spiritual role, in carnivals and feast days of Colombia's majority mestizo (part-Indian, part-European) population. Colombians adore such fiestas and there is likely to be one nearly everyday of the year in some part of the country. The creation of masks for such festive occasions has consequently become a highly esteemed art form and the masks are prized.

Above. Eduardo Muñoz Lora using barniz de Pasto—*a colorful finish— in his workshop. Pasto, Nariño.*

Left. The figure of a peasant woman carved in wood and covered with Pasto varnish. Eduardo Muñoz Lora, Sandoná, Nariño.

Right. Traditional Indian stool from Putumayo, carved from a single block of wood and elaborately decorated with Pasto varnish. Eduardo Muñoz Lora, Sandoná, Nariño.

Pasto varnish or barniz de Pasto, *named for the town in which it was first made, is an ornamental surface made from the Mopa Mopa tree. Although given its name by the Spanish, it was used for centuries before their arrival by the local Indians. The Indians took balls of resin from the leaf bud of the tree, dyed them in different colors, and then varnished domestic utensils with the resulting substance.*

Opposite: A Black Virgin Mary and Child. The figure is carved from wood and decorated with barniz de Pasto *and the "wheat/ barley stalk" technique. Pasto, Nariño.*

Above left. A nativity scene has been etched through pyrography—burning with a hot instrument—inside this wooden coffer. It is also decorated with wheat or barley stalk appliqués. Carlos Sánchez, Nariño.

Above right. A country vignette in wheat or barley stalks decorates this wooden vase. Sandoná, Nariño.

Wheat or barley stalks are attached to the surface of an object with homemade glue, following an already drawn outline. This is a popular craft and is used by artisans throughout the country to decorate utilitarian objects.

Previous pages.
Page 184. This wooden shoe-shine box reveals the somewhat eccentric taste of its owner. Atlántico.

Page 185. A balsa wood sailboat. Caribbean Coast.

Top. A painted toy ship. Tumaco, Nariño.

Center. Little wooden requintos— guitars with five double strings— are carried by the "cowboys" of the Colombian plains, so that they can entertain themselves on long trips away from home. The resonance box of this one is made from the back of an armadillo. The requintos have a higher, thinner sound than the similar tiple guitar with four sets of three strings. Los Llanos.

Bottom. Wooden toys carved on a lathe and decorated with burned or incised bands. Chiquinquirá, Boyacá.

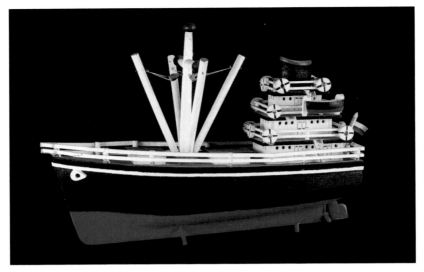

Opposite. Young shaman apprentices carve these boats when they are first initiated. The figures on board symbolize the spirits the new shaman will be working with. Later, he will carve a walking stick for use in rituals, and a stool. Noanamá and Emberá Indians, Chocó.

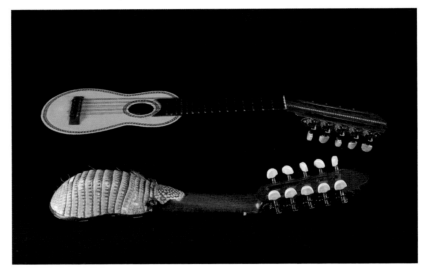

Top. Miniature ornamental cutlery carved in orange wood. Obonuco, Nariño.

Bottom. Wooden utensils— spoons, rollers, and whisks— on sale at a village market. Tolima.

Opposite. Wooden cheese presses. These delicate machines are made by cabinetmakers and used to separate the whey from the curd. Excellent cheeses are produced in the region around the nation's capital, Bogotá.

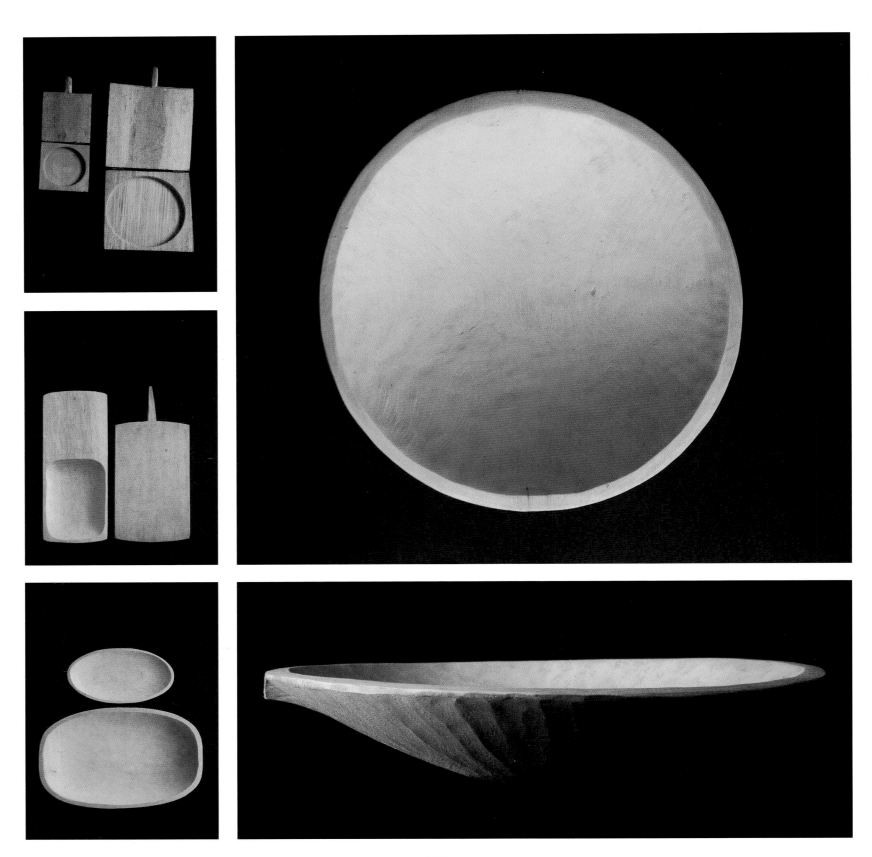

Opposite. Wooden bowls, boards, and dishes. The various woods from which they have been made, usually a white wood, were selected for their impermeable and durable qualities. Manizales, Caldas.

Top right. Bowls turned on a lathe in muello and cedar wood. They have been sanded and finished with a thin layer of paraffin. Galería Deimos, Bogotá.

Bottom right. Salad bowl and servers carved in oak. The handles of the servers are decorated with horn and silver. Galería Deimos, Bogotá.

Opposite. Interior patio of a wooden house. Salamina, Caldas.

Inland, to the northwest of Colombia, is the coffee-growing region. It spans three departments, Caldas, Risaralda, and Quindío and is an area of mountainous, plantation-covered slopes. Just to the north is Antioquia, a department that still retains a strong European flavor. Over the years, this character has filtered down somewhat to the coffee-growing region, and is known as the "Antioquean colonization." The delicate wooden flourishes, balconies, and courtyards of Spanish Colonial architecture can be seen in Antioquia but also in the towns and villages to the south, even though it was not originally heavily colonized by the Spaniards. Carvers, such as Orrego and Tangarife, have perpetuated these European traditions but made use of the native resources and local culture.

Following pages. Painted wood ceilings worked in geometrical shapes that form recognizable outlines: flowers, leaves, fans, circles, diamonds, squares. They are finished with central rosettes, also carved in wood. Quindío.

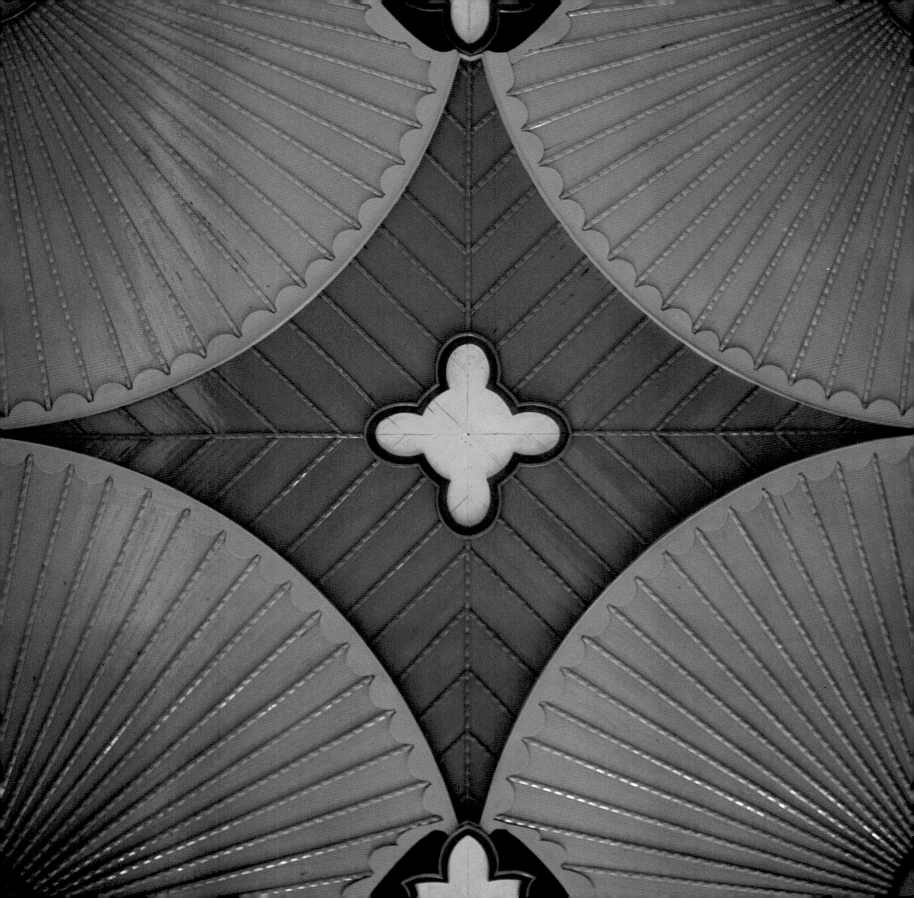

Above. Panpipes and other traditional musical instruments of the Andes. Manizales, Caldas.

Left. Birdcage made of caña brava inhabited by decorative ceramic birds. Boyacá.

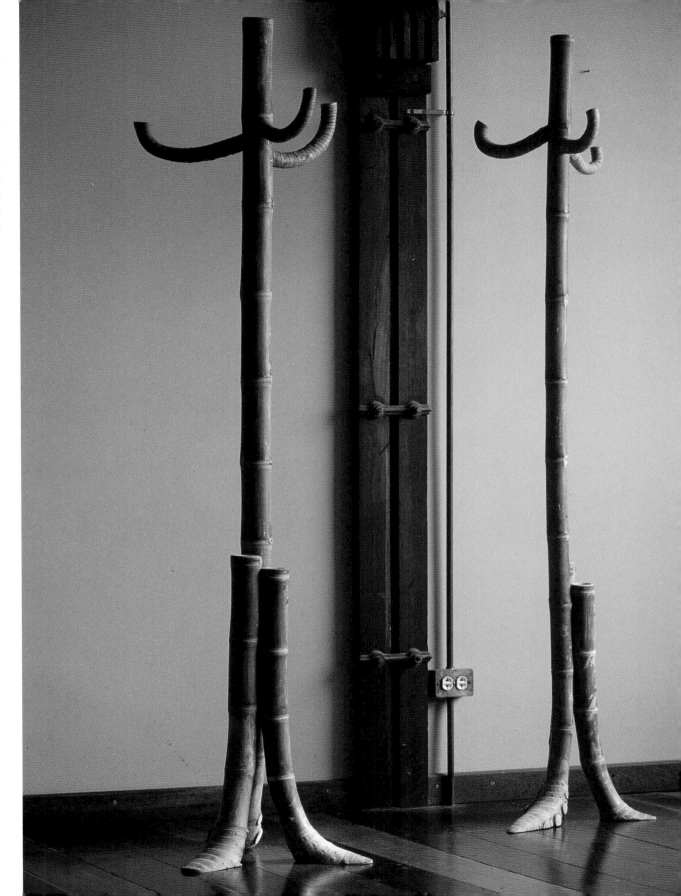

Hatrack in bamboo. Marcelo Villegas, Manizales, Caldas.

Caña brava—or wild cane, is a straight-stalked grass that grows wild in Colombia. The stalks are cut when they are mature and are stored in the shade so that they do not dry out. The plant is particularly suited to basketry, but a number of other objects are also made from it: toys, flutes, whistles, vases, lamps, and chests.

Top. Cutlery and holders made of guadua—a tropical American bamboo. Germán Rubio, La Calera, Cundinamarca.

Bottom. Guadua containers made on a lathe. Germán Rubio, La Calera, Cundinamarca.

Opposite.
Top. Grain containers made of guadua. Marcelo Villegas, Manizales, Caldas.

Left. Flutes of caña brava. Various regions.

Top center. Guadua vase. Alejandro Cabo, Bogotá.

Bottom center. A sturdy stool in guadua and wood. Alejandro Cabo, Bogotá.

Right. Marimba—or xylophone in palm wood, with resonance pipes of guadua. Guapi, Cauca.

The table of the marimba or xylophone is made up of two pieces of guadua or resistant wood, six and one-half feet long, separated at each end by transverse pieces, one of ten and the other of thirty inches. Coconut bagasse pieces cushion the blows of the twenty-four graduated tucuma wood boards, which are distributed along the center of the structure and are suspended symmetrically over twenty-four guadua pipes. Each one still has its characteristic knots and pulp on the inside, with the upper part perforated. The boards are hit with sets of hard wooden sticks with a rubber ball fixed on the end. The marimba may be suspended or set on wooden legs.

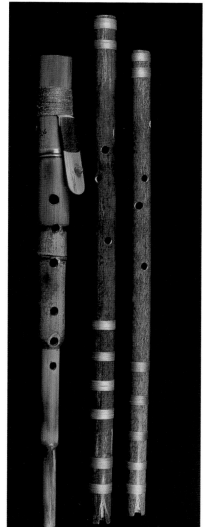

Above. Bedroom with shuttered windows and guadua *and canvas lamps. The upper ventilation is in* macana *wood and the general structure of the roof is in* guadua. *Simón Vélez, lamps designed by Ezequiel Alarcón, Barichara, Santander.*

Opposite. Lamp base and shade support carved in bamboo. Ezequiel Alarcón, Barichara, Santander.

LEATHER

Pre-Columbian societies—as most early cultures—used animal skins for clothing, blankets, footwear, and as containers to hold grains and liquids. Since leather is a highly perishable medium, few vestiges of this ancient craft remain today, although its use among indigenous Colombians, who still maintain many of the craft traditions of their pre-Hispanic ancestors, is a strong indication of an early leatherworking tradition. The desert-dwelling Wayuu people of the Guajira, for example, who continue to weave and make pots much as they did centuries ago, also tan and process animal skins for sandal soles, shoulder bags, and chairbacks.

The arrival of the Spanish in South America, did, however, dramatically change the leather industry, for they brought with them not only horses and cattle and well-developed leatherworking skills—but a taste for elaborately worked and painted leather furniture. The Spanish style in furniture of the sixteenth and seventeenth centuries was largely Renaissance in inspiration—the wood was dark and elaborately carved and the shapes were of massive proportions. Sumptuously etched, embossed, engraved, carved, polychromed, and pyrogravured leather was often stretched over wooden frames to make chair seats and backs. The various skills necessary for turning the tropical rain forests and mountainous lands of South

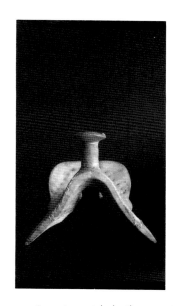

A western-style leather saddletree. Salamina, Caldas.

Opposite. A pre-Columbian clay pot with a leather cover, which protects it and makes it easier to carry. A.D. XV century. Tierradentro, Cauca.

America into a prosperous "New Granada" were imported and taught to local artisans. *Obradores*—or European guild-like workshops, opened throughout the newly colonized territories, particularly in the thriving settlements of Quito in Ecuador and Pasto and Popayán in Colombia.

The "monk's" or "monastery" chair was a particularly popular feature of the New Granada salon. These Italian Renaissance-style chairs—perhaps more appropriate for a monastic cell than the tropical, sun-flooded homes of the Caribbean—had calfskin backs that were embossed, often with the owner's coat-of-arms or an ecclesiastic or civic seal. The leather was usually further enriched with color. The Colombian version of the chair was not as ornate, the wood less carved and there was little, if any, bronze ornamentation. The forbidding shape was softened somewhat in later models—armrests began to curve slightly and the head support was often carved in the shape of a shell or open fan. European styles, then, merged with local styles and tastes to create furniture ideally suited to the South American climates.

Particularly fine examples of these chairs emerged from the workshops of Pasto—a small town in southern Colombia, whose carpenters developed a distinctive, colorful wood varnish or—*barniz de Pasto*— made from the resin of the *mopa* tree.

The most singular leather article to be identified with an entire region and, perhaps, even the whole nation, is the *carriel* of Antioquia—a Creole adaptation of the European saddlebag. The origin of the *carriel* and the roots of its peculiar name have been the subject of numerous investigations. Some claim the word *carriel* originated in Ecuador or Venezuela; others trace its roots to the English term "carry all." During the Colonial period it was called a *guarniel*, a name that is still used in regions today; from this term comes the name for the workshops where it is made: *guarniderias*. What is certain is that the *carriel* has been in use since Antioquia was colonized, and was carried by the *arrieros* —or muleteers—on their trips off into the mountains.

"The *carriel* carries the soul of its owner" is a line from a popular ballad and conveys some of the significance of this shoulder bag to Colombian rural people. The *carriel* must transport everything needed for living in the Andes, items so diverse and varied as a folding razor, tobacco, ointments, dice and a deck of cards, to religious or magical objects, such as oxeyes—large round seeds used as amulets, cloths stamped with religious images, and the figure of Saint Genevieve, a popular icon in Antioquia.

There are four typical *carriel* designs: the *jericoano*, manufactured in Envigado, Sabaneta, and Medellín; the *sampedreño* from Medellín and

Leather and wood chairs at an outdoor café before opening time. Jardín, Antioquia.

Wooden bed and night tables covered with stamped leather. Cauca.

Opposite. Toy horses in wood and leather. Pereira, Risaralda.

Envigado; the *envigadeño* and the *Amalfitano,* which have all but vanished today. The *jericoano* has a rounded shape and is closed with a tongue or fastener that passes through a leather loop. The *sampedreño* is somewhat smaller than the *jericoano* and is usually used by older men. The *envigadeño* and *amalfitano* are considered old-fashioned and not produced much any more. The *carriel* is always made of leather and has a series of compartments and divisions among which there is at least one secret pocket. The front of the *carriel* is made of cowhide with patent leather details and colorful stitching; it is multi-gusseted, and looks somewhat like a billows; it can be rounded or squared.

Traditionally, only men manufacture *carriels*; women help in secondary chores such as handsewing details, gluing, or affixing the metallic overlays that sometimes adorn the long shoulderbag.

Another accoutrement to the Andean dweller was the *petacas* or cowhide trunks; these were once standard pieces of equipment for travelers crossing the mountainous areas of the country, but are now somewhat obsolete.

The *barqueño* falls somewhere between a leather-covered coffer and a large chest; it is actually a small desk or portable accounting table, that was used as a basic fixture in home decoration and could be packed up to carry on

expeditions and military campaigns, including those of Simón Bolívar, as Gabriel García Márquez describes in *The General and His Labyrinth*. *Bargueños* are delicate and finely wrought pieces of furniture; the solidly built chest is full of a series of small drawers with elegant drawer pulls and rests on separate stand. The doors, with silver hardware and mother-of-pearl, tortoise shell, ivory, and precious wood encrustations, can fold up and become all but impenetrable.

The lowlands to the east of the Andes, Llanos Orientales—or Eastern Plains—are ranching country. A range of leather products are made here to service this industry, including hand-twisted and braided lassos, whips, reins, chaps, tack, and saddlery.

The machete and its characteristic sheath serve almost as symbols for Colombia, since they have proved indispensable to the progress of the country. With the machete, Colombians have opened roads, cleared undergrowth, settled entire regions, performed the chores necessary for everyday rural life, and fought wars of independence. The machete, hanging from the waist of the *campesino*—or farmer, catching the sunlight on its steel blade or sheathed in its beautifully worked leather case, is one of the most familiar of rural Colombian sights.

Leather-and-wood percussion instruments, such

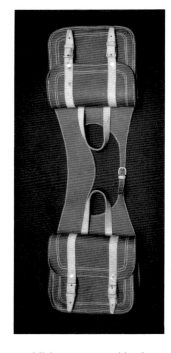

Saddlebags in tanned leather. Quindío.

Opposite. A leather carriel—*the traditional Antioquean shoulder bag, with a cover made from the skin of a wild cat and edging in patent leather. Jericó, Antioquia.*

as the bongo drum, were brought over by the Africans, who eventually settled along the Caribbean coast of Colombia. They continue to be made with great skill and the instrument has become an integral part of the country's musical tradition.

Beginning in the 1960s, saddleries in some artisan centers shifted their production from tack to smaller leather goods, including handbags, attaché cases, duffel bags, and suitcases. This change breathed new life into the industry, placing it in an important position among leather production centers and providing a foundation for a prosperous Colombian small leather goods industry.

Creative interior designers have devised new uses for leather, including floor coverings, geometrically designed throw rugs, and comfortable, elegant furniture. Over the last few years, the leather industry has enjoyed tremendous popularity domestically. Small and large manufacturers have now started to look overseas, and by participating in specialized trade fairs, Colombian manufacturers have been able to make their quality production known to the most demanding international markets. Desktop articles, belts, bags, and purses, together with larger leather goods and clothing, have become one of the country's principal export categories.

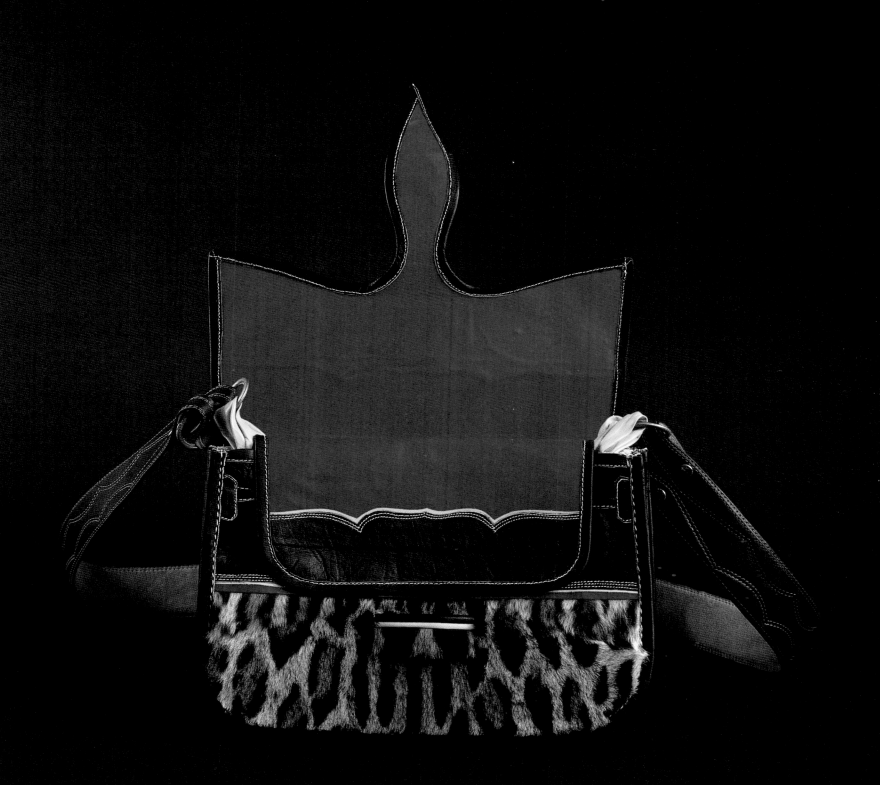

Left. The wooden frame of this chest was covered with magnificent, embossed leather. The top, attached with silver hinges, is finished with barniz de Pasto—a traditional Colombian varnish drawn from tree resin. This impressive piece served as a desk at home, and as a portable office during military campaigns. Simón Bolívar, El Libertador, carried a similar piece with him throughout his South American campaigns. XVIII century. Popayán, Cauca.

*Opposite.
Top. A trunk covered with engraved, embossed leather on a wooden structure with carved legs. XVIII century. Bogotá.*

Below. The leather covering this trunk is held in place with prominent copper studs. XIX century. Bogotá.

Top left. Monastery chairs upholstered in embossed and Pasto-varnished leather. These splendid pieces are characteristic examples of Colonial furniture. XVIII century. Popayán, Cauca.

Bottom left. A wood and leather chair in the Spanish style; the undecorated trunk on the ground—notably less grand than the other chests shown—is extremely sturdy and was intended for transport by mule. XIX century. Popayán, Cauca.

Opposite. Detail of the back of a monastery chair in embossed, polychrome leather. Pasto, Nariño.

Above. Leather machete sheaths made of calfskin. The indispensible machete is used throughout the country for farmwork, to clear jungle paths, and also, at times, as weapons. Zipaquirá, Cundinamarca.

Left. Cowhide chaps worn by cowboys of the Colombian plains. East of the Andes is a huge stretch of lowlands, crossed by several rivers, that is devoted almost exclusively to cattle and sheep grazing. This industry is an important part of the country's economy—and the rugged character of the plains's cowboy is the source of many legends. Los Llanos.

Right. Cowboys herd their cattle with these crude leather lariats, made from twisted strips of hide that have been softened with beef fat and dried in the sun. Los Llanos.

Above. Tack shed with leather saddles. Caldas.

Opposite. A light leather saddle. Medellín, Antioquia.

Soon after the arrival of the Spaniards—who brought horses to South America—a leather-working industry began to develop in Colombia. Belts, thongs, saddles, *traveling trunks, and many other equestrian items were produced in Colonial workshops.*

Following pages.
Page 216. These unusual floor tiles are made from thick, unrefined squares of leather. Bogotá.

Page 217. A cowhide rug. Chía, Cundinamarca.

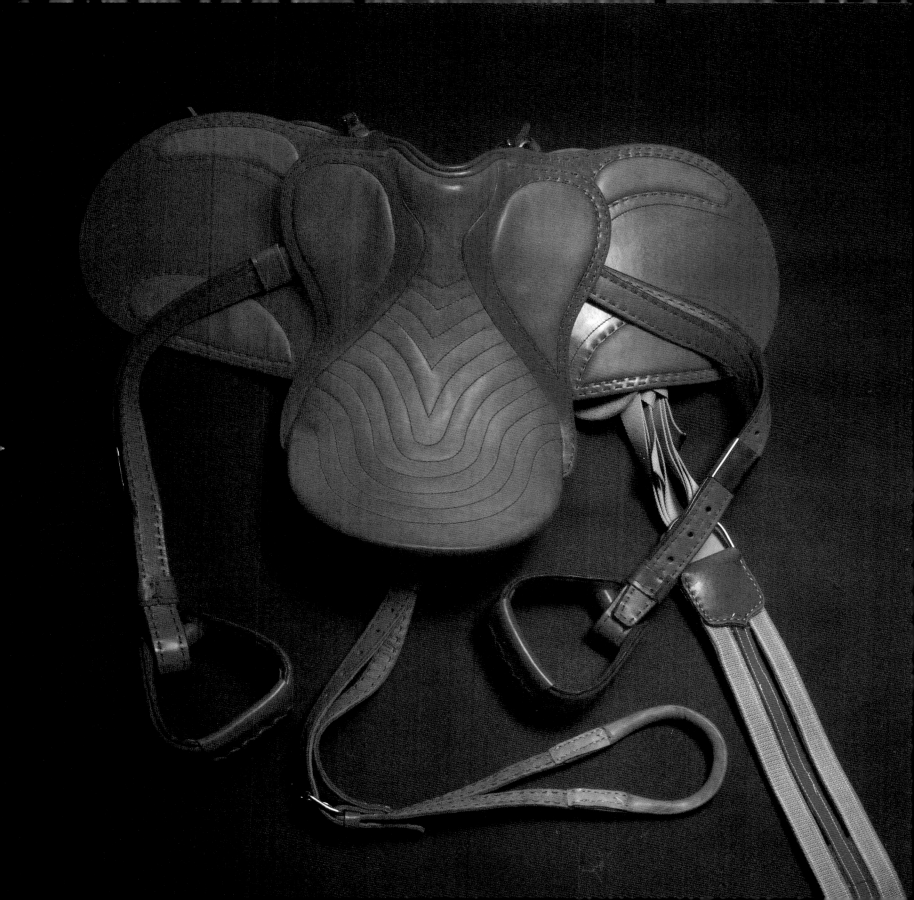

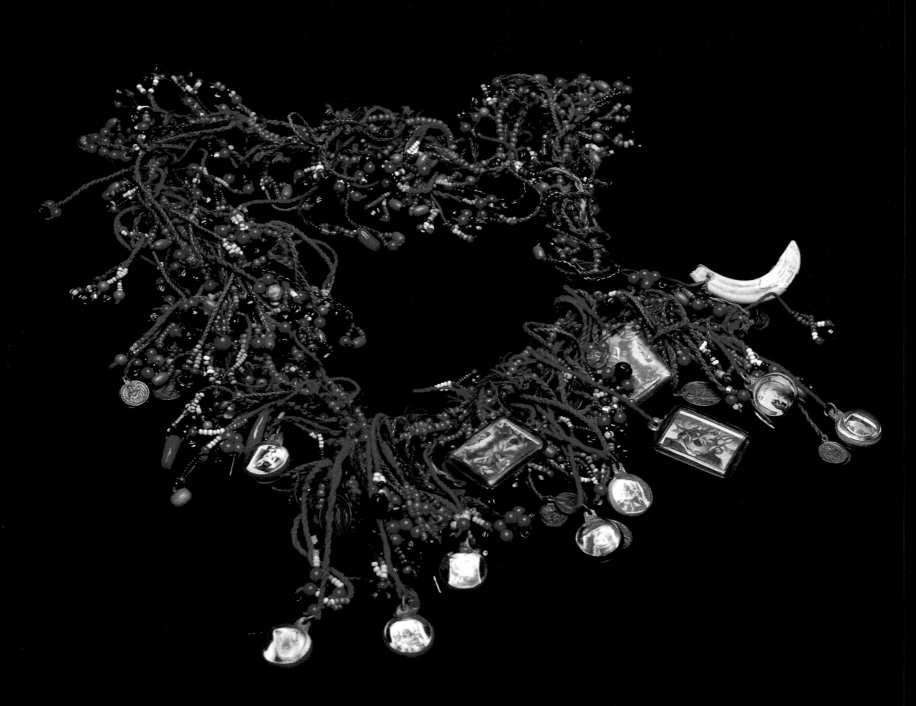

MISCELLANEOUS

From an egg basket of armadillo shell to a headdress of scarab wings and bird feathers, Colombian artisans seek to meet both the everyday and ceremonial needs of their communities with whatever material is available.

The indigenous people of Colombia, who still retain strong ties to the natural world, are particularly creative in drawing on their surroundings. They use seeds, bird feathers, insect wings, animal bones, and fangs to adorn themselves for rituals and ceremonies. Aboriginal communities of the Amazon use feathers from the resplendently plumed birds of their rain forest—macaws, royal cranes, toucans—for ceremonial headdresses. For them feathers are symbols of status, as well as an identity sign for each tribe. The number and flamboyancy of the feathers worn can clearly denote the person's rank within the hierarchy of a group. Splendid feather headdresses, body paint gleaned from the colors of the earth and plant life, necklaces, and rattles are all a part of ritual attire. Feathers are also woven to make crowns or flat combs and, mixed with bone, boar or ocelot fangs, or stone and seed beads, they serve as necklaces. These rattles and necklaces are not solely decorative but serve a musical function among many of Colombia's traditional cultures. Worn around the ankles, calves, waist, arms, and necks of ceremonial

An egg carrier made from the armor-like shell of an armadillo. These odd-looking creatures are found in northern Colombia, where they are hunted for their meat and their versatile shells. Magdalena.

Opposite. Necklace decorated with charms and beads to protect the wearer and ward off evil. Guambiano Indians, Cauca.

dancers, they rattle and rustle as the dancer moves rhythmically, imitating the uproarious clamoring, whistling, blowing, rainfall, and thunder of nature.

Another of the magnificently worked natural products is the calabash gourd. Calabash trees grow profusely along the banks of the Cauca River and in the department of Tolima. In Valle del Cauca, calabash halves are used to package *manjar blanco*, a creamy fudge made of milk and sugar, which is typical to the region and extremely popular. The gourds most appropriate for decorating are those that have reached full maturity before being harvested; unripe fruit is too soft. Even so, a calabash that is to be decorated must first be thoroughly dried, which takes four to five days; then it is sanded and finally either painted or carved. Sometimes, the artisan follows an established pattern; at other times, the design is improvised creating a freeform interpretation of current styles. Some etched calabash gourds are simply decorative accessories; but others serve as ladles, bowls, or receptacles.

Human figures, fauna, flowers, scenes from daily life, leaves, and stylized borders with spiral motifs are characteristic of the drawings seen on these gourds. On the Atlantic Coast, in the city of Sincelejo, the etchings on a calabash shell frequently narrate the *corraleja*—a popular regional sport, the bullfight. Other scenes are associated with cattle ranching, farming, and harvest time. Such stories are told in sequence on the outer shell of the calabash, a sort of chronicle of popular life. In Jamundi, in the department of Valle del Cauca, artisans focus on the environment, depicting natural motifs rather than specific scenes.

The entire coconut palm tree—its fruit, leaves, and trunk—can be used to manufacture countless articles and substances for everyday use. The fronds of the palm are used to thatch houses and make fences. Its limbs can be woven into floor coverings, baskets, hats, brooms, brushes, and fans. The flowers and roots are used to make brooms and brushes. The husks of the fronds are often shaped into lamp shades, slippers, baskets, and even clothing and blankets. The outer covering of the fruit can be transformed into rugs, ropes, and brushes. And the hard shell makes lovely buttons, combs, cups, flowerpots, spoons, and toys. Even the old trunks are put to use as round logs for civil and marine construction.

A miniature carving made on a lathe in a palm seed known as "vegetable ivory." Chiquinquirá.

Artisans from the Guajira perforate the shell with a conical needle, backwards and forwards, and use the punctured vessel as a colander.

Spanish artisans of the middle ages inlaid furniture with delicate horn and tortoise shell patterns. This decorative tradition traveled to the Americas during the Colonial period, supplementing the local uses for armadillo and tortoise shell and the horn of wild boar. As cattle ranching increased in South America, horn became more plentiful, and its uses expanded to include boxes, coffers, *bargueños*, and picture frames. The techniques for inlaying with shell and horn could also be applied to other materials. Ivory, bone, and mother-of-pearl proved ideal for this kind of intricate work.

Such seemingly unartistic articles as bone and palm tree roots can, in the hands of an ingenious artisan, be transformed into objects of beauty that enrich our lives and ease our daily chores.

Opposite. Detail of a bone-inlaid coffer. XVII century. Bogotá.

Pre-Columbian necklaces with
bone beads, button-shaped shells,
and snail shells. Different cultures.

Pre-Columbian necklaces of bone
beads, animal fangs, and shells,
resting on a ceramic vase.
Tayrona culture.

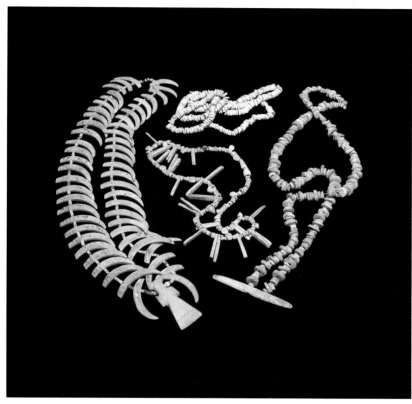

Pre-Columbian stone necklaces.
Atlántico.

Pre-Columbian beads cut from
stones and set on a silver hoop.
Atlántico.

An ornament of scarab wings and bird feathers. Guaviare.

Left and right. Feathers from exotic birds of the Amazon jungle—macaws, parrots, and toucans—are used in splendid ceremonial Indian headdresses. Putumayo and Amazonas.

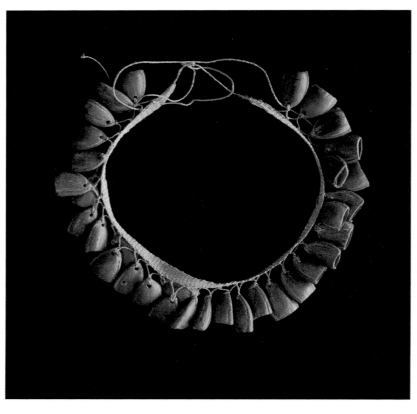
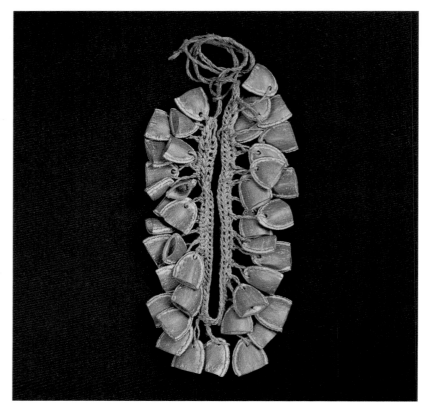

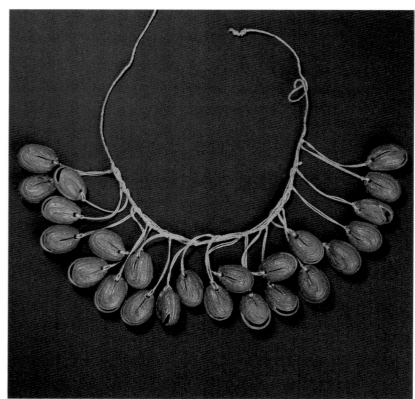

Left. Seed rattles are used by many of Colombia's Indians in ceremonies and rituals conducted to help ensure a successful crop, send off a family member to the world of spirits, bless a new communal house, or inititiate youths into the social and religious life of a community. These celebrations almost always involve dancing. Festooned with rattles around their waists, necks, arms, and legs, the dancers rythmically move and stamp their feet, echoing with the rattles the sounds of nature—the rustling of leaves or the "music of water"— and creating a lively, festive din.

Right. A ceremonial feather, bone, and seed headdress. Vaupés.

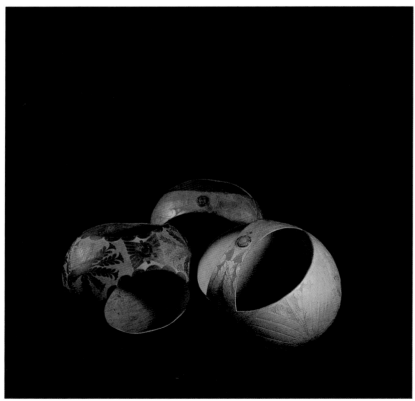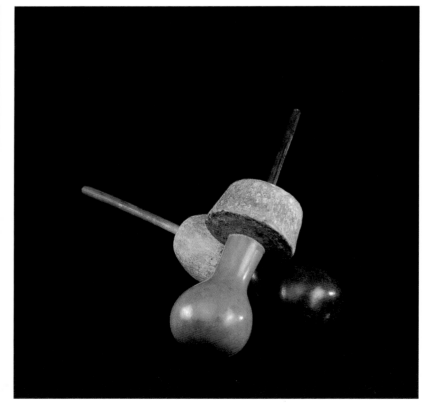

Left.
Top left and right. Calabash containers and rattles. The decoration of this shell includes both figurative motifs and scenes from daily life, including cattle rearing and festive celebrations. Córdoba.

Bottom left. Basket-like gourd carriers. Córdoba.

Bottom right. These calabash containers are seen in the hands of male Kogui Indians at almost all times. The shells contain a lime paste that is removed with the thin sticks attached to the tops and then chewed with coca leaves—a custom similar to chewing tobacco. The sticks are wiped off on the neck of the shell, before being stuck back inside, and the resulting residue gradually builds up into a thick white rim, as can be seen here. Magdalena.

Right. Maracas—rattle-like instruments made from calabash shells. Atlántico.

The calabash is usually carved with knives, awls, burins, and augers. Although gourd carving originated among Colombia's Indian population, it is now an art form practiced as well in many of the country's Black communities.

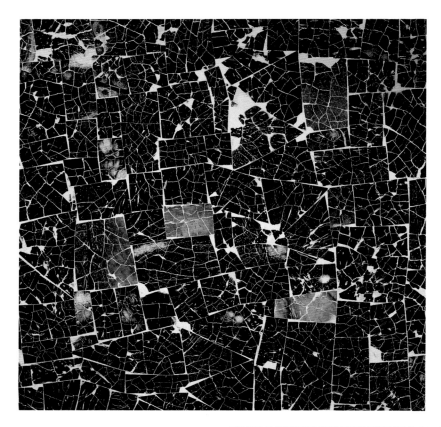

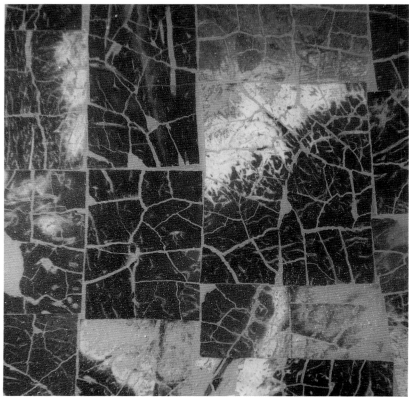

Details of coconut overlaid on wooden surfaces, mainly used in furniture, frames, and chests. Ibagué, Tolima.

Opposite page. Concrete-filled coconut finials top the handrail of a staircase. Marcelo Villegas, Manizales, Caldas.

Top and bottom. Horn boxes and cutlery made by artisans along the Caribbean Coast.

Opposite. Detail of a table inlaid with horn. Manizales, Caldas.

Cattle horn has been used for creating artifacts in South America for centuries. Its main component—keratin—is an insoluble, fibrous protein that makes it an ideal, durable medium.

First the horn is soaked in water to soften and remove the bony interior. Then, to make the empty horn more malleable, it is boiled in water or industrial oil until it can be handled, sectioned, extended, pressed, or cut. The lovely burnish of these pieces comes from rigorous polishing with sandpaper or a polisher.

GLOSSARY

ADOBE: a mixture of mud and occasionally straw, molded into the shapes of bricks and dried in the open air; adobe bricks are used to build all types of walls.

ALPARGATAS: sandal-like footwear with cloth toecaps and pita fiber soles; they are tied around the ankle with cotton ribbons.

ATILLO: a rustic leather suitcase. In the past it was used to carry belongings on the backs of donkeys and mules.

BAHAREQUE: a masonry system composed of a strong, woven cane structure covered with vegetable fibers and mud.

BARGUEÑO: a Colonial piece of wood furniture with drawers and cabinets for storing personal objects, papers, and desk accessories. They were usually carved and adorned with brightly colored, painted motifs and gold leafing. Some were elaborately inlaid or finished with *barniz de Pasto*.

CANTARO: a large ceramic vessel with a narrow mouth and large belly. It can have one or two handles and is used for storing and transporting liquids.

CAPADOR: pre-Hispanic musical instrument with several varying sizes of caña brava or guadua canutos. Also

referred to as panpipes.

CARGUERA: a large *mochila* or shoulder bag used for carrying heavy objects.

CARRIEL: a travel bag (also called a *garriel*) carried as a shoulder bag with various compartments for papers and money, widely used in Antioquia and Caldas.

CATARIJANO: indigenous packaging made of woven palm fronds and used for storing and transporting fruits and other foodstuffs.

CAZABE: a bread or large pancake common to various parts of South America made of manioc or bitter cassava root flour.

CHAGRA: a farm or vegetable garden located near a dwelling.

CHICA: red dye prepared from pieces of ground pottery dissolved in water. This indigenous procedure is used by artisans in Boyacá to decorate or adorn pieces of pottery.

CHICHA: alcoholic beverage derived from fermenting corn in sugar water.

CHINCHORRO: a light-weight hammock woven of tightly twisted yarn. It is the bed commonly used by many Colombian Indians.

CHIPIRE: a small spiral-shaped disk used as the spherical base for some woven objects.

CHIRCAL: tileworks or place where bricks and roofing tiles are manufactured.

CHIVA: popular mode of transportation very much like a bus which is used in various regions of Colombia to carry people or cargo. The body of these vehicles is usually profusely decorated with landscapes and other art motifs. Also known as *bus escalera* because of the ladder on the outside.

CHUMBE: cotton belt or girdle with brightly colored woven figures.

CONGA: a type of drum made of leather and wood.

COTIZAS: type of sandal, very common in rural areas, made of cloth with a sturdy sole.

ENJALMA: type of saddle for beasts of burden. In the coffee-growing region it is made of pita fiber.

FALSA FILIGRANA: imitation or false filigree, a pre-Columbian technique of casting metals, which reproduces the appearance of twisted and soldered gold wires.

GUALDRAPA: brightly colored

woolen rugs which protect and adorn the backs of mules and horses. Today they are also used as floor rugs.

GUAYUCO: a loin cloth.

GÜERREGUE: a palm tree whose fiber is used by the Noanamá Indians for weaving baskets. The weave is so tight that these baskets can carry water.

JAIBANA: shaman to the Emberá indigenous communities of the Chocó jungle. It is said that they possess magical powers.

MALOCA: indigenous dwelling used by some Amazon tribes. It has large proportions and is covered by a roof and walls of woven palm fronds. The front of the maloca is straight, while the back is rounded and gives the roof its characteristic semi-conical shape. Several family units share a *maloca*.

MAMBEO: the process of chewing coca leaves.

MARACAS: musical instrument made from the gourd of the totumo or calabash tree with capacho seeds inside and a handle on the outside. When shaken they produce a rasping sound. They are also part of the ritual and ceremonial paraphernalia used by indigenous tribes and are often beautifully decorated.

METATE: elongated rectangular stone on which corn and other grains are ground using another stone.

MOCHILA: type of shoulder bag characteristic of some pre-Hispanic communities, woven of different fibers and in various shapes and sizes. Its use has become common in all regions of Colombia. It is used as a handbag, to carry personal objects and also for heavy objects.

MOCHILON: extremely large pita fiber mochila used for carrying heavy objects.

MOLA: a square piece of cloth, created by the Cuna Indians with motifs which reproduce zoomorphic and purely geometric figures in varied colors.

MOYO: a large clay pot used in processing mineral salt extracted from salt mines.

NASA: art of fishing which consists of employing a cylinder of woven reeds with a sort of funnel directed toward the inside of one of its bases and closed with a top on the other end for emptying it.

PLATO DE BAILAR LOZA: a ceramic plate used in hand-turning clay vessels.

POPORO: a receptacle made out of a calabash gourd in which the indigenous people store powered lye used as a catalyzing agent in *mambeo*. The ancient Colombian cultures also made them in gold.

REQUINTO: a ten-stringed musical instrument similar to the *tiple* or a small guitar.

RUANA: a woolen poncho-like garment that is closed front and back and open on the sides. It has a hole for the head and falls loosely from the shoulders around the body.

SEBUCAN: a flexible, cylindrical juice press that is used for extracting the prussic acid from the manioc root.

SIIRA: a sash or girdle used for tying the *guayuco*.

TAPIA PISADA: an Andean technique used for building walls which involves mixing mud with straw, pita fiber, and dung. Usually it is used on top of foundations of stone or some other erosion resistant material.

TOTUMA: semi-spherical receptacle made out of the fruit of the calabash or totumo tree.

TRAPICHE: sugar mill where the juice of the sugar cane is extracted.

TUMBAGA: brittle metallic alloy made of gold and an equal or lesser amount of copper. It was one of the most widely used alloys in pre-Columbian metallurgy.

YAGE: hallucinogenic beverage consumed during sacred indigenous ceremonies.

ACKNOWLEDGMENTS

PHOTOGRAPHERS

The editor wishes to thank the following institutions
for providing historical and technical information, and
for permission to photograph their collections:
MUSEUM OF POPULAR ARTS AND TRADITIONS,
GOLD MUSEUM, CHICO MUSEUM,
MUSEUM OF COLONIAL ART, NATIONAL MUSEUM,
NATIONAL ANTHROPOLOGY MUSEUM,
ARCHAEOLOGY MUSEUM CASA DEL MARQUES DE SAN JORGE,
MUSEUM OF RELIGIOUS ART,
COLOMBIAN REGIONAL COSTUMES MUSEUM, and
CRAFTS OF COLOMBIA in Bogotá;
ANTHROPOLOGY MUSEUM OF CALDAS UNIVERSITY,
MUSEUM OF RELIGIOUS ART, CASA FRANCISCO JOSE DE CALDAS,
TOMAS CIPRIANO DE MOSQUERA MUSEUM,
and MOSQUERA ARCHIVES in Popayán.

He also wants to acknowledge the valuable collaboration
of GALERIA CANO,
and Galerías ALONSO ARTE and DEIMOS in Bogotá.

Thanks to all the people who,
either working for the aforementioned institutions,
or from their homes and private collections,
offered valuable information and allowed us to photograph
many of the pieces shown in this book.
We especially want to mention
Guillermo Cano Mejía, Ligia de Wiesner, Pablo Solano,
Cecilia Iregui de Holguín, Guillermo Cano Varón, Clemencia Plazas,
Ana María Falchetti, Cristina Moreno, Alonso Restrepo,
María Caridad de Restrepo, Poli Mallarino,
Jaime Botero, Cecilia Duque, María Teresa Marroquín, Gonzalo Ariza,
Manuel Lorenzo Villegas, Nebe Herrera, Myriam de Villamizar,
Alvaro Chávez, Silvia Gómez, María Cristina Padilla,
Pilar Bermúdez, Olga de Amaral, Elvira de Saa, Moncha Mejía,
Enrique Grau, Diego Castrillón, Néstor Tobón,
and the artisans of our towns and cities, who patiently and generously
answered every question and showed us their most prized artifacts.

Note: the letters beside the page numbers correspond to the placement
of the photograph on each page, from top to bottom and left to right.

JOSE FERNANDO MACHADO:
Cover, Back cover, Endpapers.
Page: 1, 2, 3, 5, 17, 24, 30, 31,
32, 35, 36, 37, 39, 40, 41, 42,
43, 47 b, 48, 49, 50, 52, 55 a,
58, 60, 61, 62 a, c, e, 63, 66, 67,
71, 72, 73, 74, 75, 76, 77, 78,
79, 82, 83, 91, 92, 93, 94, 95,
102 a, 103 b, 104, 106, 108, 109,
112, 114 a, 115, 116 b, 117, 119
a, c, 122, 123, 125, 126, 130,
131, 132, 133, 134, 136 a, 137,
138, 139, 143, 144, 146, 148,
149, 150, 152 b, 153, 154,155,
156 a, 157,158, 159, 160 a, 161,
163, 164, 165, 168 a, b, 169,
172, 173, 174, 175, 176, 177,
178 c, 179 c, 180 a, 181, 182,
183, 184, 185, 186 a, b, 187,
188, 189, 191, 198, 199 b, c, d,
e, 202, 207, 208, 211, 212 b,
213, 216, 217, 219, 222 b, 224,
225, 226, 228, 229, 232.

JORGE EDUARDO ARANGO:
12, 33 e, 50 b, 54, 57, 59, 78 b,
83, 110, 116 a, 118, 124, 135,
136 c, 147 b, 151 b, 166 a, 168
c, 196 a, 199 a, 204 a, 209, 223
b, 230 c, 231.

DIEGO MIGUEL GARCES: 33,
64, 65, 90, 96, 97, 100, 101,
113, 127, 129, 142, 152 a,160 b,
170, 171, 180 b, 204 b, 210.

DIEGO SAMPER: 22, 44, 45, 53,
62 b, d, f, 63, 84, 145, 147 a,
151 a, 156 b, 162, 166 b, 167,
190, 196 b, 197, 203, 205, 206,
212 a, 215, 221, 230 a, b, 233.

PILAR GOMEZ: 15, 19, 68 a, 70,
87, 102 b, 166 c, 178 a, 186 c,
201, 222 a, 227, 228 b, c.

OSCAR MONSALVE: 34, 55 b,
80, 81, 111 b, 178 b, 179 a.

ALFREDO PINZON: 56, 69, 86,
88, 89, 128, 220.

JORGE GAMBOA: 23, 25, 26,
27, 28, 29.

JUAN CAMILO SEGURA: 38, 51,
111 a, 141, 179 b.

LUCAS SCHMEEKLOTH: 68 b,
114 b, 120, 121.

SIMON VELEZ: 105, 107, 200,
214.

ARCHIVO VILLEGAS EDITORES:
20, 21, 46, 47, 105.

OLGA LUCIA JORDAN: 192,
193, 194, 195.

JANINE EL'GAZI: 218, 223 a.

JESUS VELEZ: 140.

BENJAMIN VILLEGAS: 99.

NELSON PINILLA: 98.

SANDRA PEÑA: 103 a.

GUSTAVO PEREZ: 119 b.

SANTIAGO HARKER: 136 b.

BIBLIOGRAPHY

ABADIA MORALES, G. *Compendio general de folklore colombiano*. Bogotá, Talleres Gráficos Banco Popular, 1983.

ACUÑA, L. A. *El arte de los indios colombianos*. Bogotá, Escuelas Gráficas Salesianas, 1935.

BALCAZAR COLLO, R. *Artesanías. Explotación indígena y desarrollo en La Guajira*. Bogotá, Ministerio de Desarrollo, 1974.

BARNEY CABRERA, E. et al. *Historia del arte colombiano*. Barcelona, Salvat Editores S. A., 1986. 6 vols.

BOLIVAR, E. "Tres culturas, tres procesos artesanales." *Boletín de antropología*. Universidad de Antioquia. Vol. 6, no. 20: 111–162.

BRANDO LEON, A. "La *Mola* en el arte de los indios Cuna." *Lámpara*, Vol. XXIV, no. 102: 11–17.

BREW, R. *El desarrollo económico de Antioquia desde la independencia hasta 1920*. Bogotá, Talleres Gráficos del Banco de la República, 1977.

BROADBENT, S. "Tradiciones cerámicas de los altiplanos de Cundinamarca y Boyacá." *Revista colombiana de antropología*. Vol. XVI, 1974: 216–243.

CENDAR. Centro de Documentación de Artesanías de Colombia. Bogotá. Documentos: Arcila Estrada, M. T. *Artesanías en el oriente antioqueño*. Medellín, 1986; Arenas, D. et al. *Investigación viejo Caldas*. Bogotá, 1986; Baquero, A. *El grabado en totumo y la talla en madera*. Bogotá, 1986; Díaz López, L. *Informe monográfico del municipio de Caldas y su técnica artesanal de tejeduría en iraca*. Bogotá, 1986; Escobar, G. *Filigrana en Santafé de Antioquia*. Bogotá, 1987; Estrada Ardila, M. T. *Artesanías de Sonsón. Tradición o necesidad*. Medellín, 1988; Fajardo, G. *Cultura material Ticuna*. Bogotá, 1986; Friedemann, N. S. de: *Estudios de negros en el litoral Pacífico colombiano*. Bogotá, 1989; Herrera, N. E. *Artesanía y organización social. Estructura de su organización gremial*. Bogotá, 1990; Otero, H. *La artesanía en el Urabá antioqueño*. Bogotá, Artesanías de Colombia, 1988; Ortiz, F. *Estudio de la cultura material y comercial entre los grupos indígenas de los Llanos Orientales*. Bogotá, 1986; Ortiz, M. de los A. *Cultura comercial y material*. Bogotá, 1987; Ramírez, M. *Introducción a las artesanías*. Bogotá, 1986; Ramírez, M. *Tejidos Wayuu*. Bogotá, 1988; Solano, P. *Artesanía Boyacense*. Bogotá, 1974; Tamayo, J. A. *El trabajo artesanal en la zona norte del litoral Pacífico*. Bogotá, 1987.

CHAVES MENDOZA, A. *Máscaras prehispánicas*. Bogotá, Centro Colombo Americano, 1984.

———."Trama y urdimbre en la historia del tejido muisca." *Lámpara*. Vol. XII, no. 94: 1–7.

CHURCH, J. D. *La agricultura y la artesanía en la utopía radical*. Bogotá, Carlos Valencia Editores, 1984.

DUQUE GOMEZ, L. *Monumentos y objetos arqueológicos*. México City, Editorial Fournier, 1955.

DUQUE GOMEZ, L. et al. "Los Quimbayas. Reseña etnográfica y arqueológica." In: *Historia de Pereira*, Ediciones el Club Rotario, 1963.

DUSSAN de REICHEL, A. "La mochila de fique." *Revista colombiana de folclor*. Vol. II, no. 5: 139–148.

FONSECA, L. and A. SALDARRIAGA, *Asentamientos y arquitectura tradicional en Colombia*. Bogotá, Ceam Ltda, 1985.

FRIEDEMANN, N. S. de. "Joyería barbacoana: artesanía en un complejo orfebre con supervivencias precolombinas."*Revista colombiana de antropología*. Vol. XVI, 1974: 56 ff.

CHAVES MENDOZA, A. *Máscaras prehispánicas*. Bogotá, Centro Colombo Americano, 1984.

GAITAN, M. M. "Historia y tejido actual de la ruana en los departamentos de Cundinamarca y Boyacá." *Boletín de información centro interamericano de artesanía y artes populares*. Cuenca. Vol. 9, 1981: 25–28.

GIL TOVAR, F. and C. ARBELAEZ CAMACHO, *El arte colonial en Colombia*. Bogotá, Editorial Sol y Luna, 1968.

GOSTAUTAS, E: *Arte Colombiano. Arte aborigen*. Bogotá, Editorial Iqueima, 1960.

HENAO, H. and P. LOMBANA, "La artesanía indígena en las selvas del Vaupés." *Boletín de antropología*. Universidad de los Andes. Vol. 6, no. 21: 101–110.

IREGUI HOLGUIN, C. *El hombre y su oficio*. Bogotá, Litografía Arco, 1983.

LABBE, A. J. *Colombia antes de Colón*. Bogotá, Carlos Valencia Editores, 1986.

MAYOR MORA, A. "Historia de la industria colombiana, 1886–1930." In: *Nueva historia de Colombia*. Vol. V. Bogotá, Editorial Planeta, 1989.

MEJIA DUQUE, J. "El carriel." *Boletín cultural y bibliográfico*. Vol. X, no. 5: 1154–1159.

MORA de JARAMILLO, Y. "Artes y artesanías populares." *Revista colombiana de folklore*. Vol. X, no. 10: 7–22.

———. "Clasificación y notas sobre técnicas y el desarrollo histórico de las artesanías colombianas." *Revista colombiana de antropología*. Vol. XVI, 1974: 283–294.

———. *Cerámica y ceramistas de Ráquira*. Bogotá, Editora Arco, 1974.

MUÑOZ, M. "La industria del sombrero de paja toquilla." *Revista colombiana de folklore*. Vol. II, no. 5: 163–168.

ORTIZ de CASTRO, B. "Historia del desarrollo artesanal en Colombia a partir de 1986." In: *Revista de la academia de historia del Meta*. Vol. 2. no. 2: 52–58.

PEÑAS GALINDO, D. E. "La orfebrería momposina: el aprendizaje de la paciencia." *Boletín Cultural y Bibliográfico*, no. 12, 1986: 45–61.

PEREZ de BARRADAS, J. *Los muiscas antes de la conquista*. Vol. I. Madrid, Consejo Superior de Investigaciones Científicas, 1950.

PINEDA GIRALDO, R. et al. *Introducción a la Colombia amerindia*. Proyecto etnológico del ICAN. Bogotá, Editorial Presencia, 1987.

PLAZAS, C. and FALCHETTI, A. M. "Patrones culturales en la orfebrería prehispánica de Colombia." In: *Metalurgia de América precolombina*. Bogotá, Universidad de los Andes, 1985: 203–215.

PREUSS, K. *Arte monumental prehistórico*. Bogotá, Escuelas Salesianas, 1931.

RAMIREZ MARTINEZ, M. "Artesanías momposinas." *Revista colombiana de folklore*. Vol. I, no. 4: 111–120.

RAYMOND, P. and B. BAYONA. "Vida y muerte del algodón y los tejidos santandereanos." *Cuadernos de agroindustria y economía rural*. Pontificia Universidad Javeriana. no. 9, 1982: 77–112.

REICHEL DOLMATOFF, G. "Colombia indígena. Período prehispánico." In: *Nueva historia de Colombia*. Bogotá, Editorial Planeta, 1989.

———. "Notas etnográficas sobre los indios del Chocó." *Revista Colombiana de Antropología*. Vol. IX, 1960: 73–158.

———. "Notas sobre alfarería del bajo Magdalena." *Revista de folklore*. no. 6, 1951: 169–176.

RIVERA, A. and L. VILLEGAS, *Iwouya. La Guajira a través del tejido*. Bogotá, Litografía Arco, 1982.

RODRIGUEZ LAMUS, L. R. *El Alfarero*. Bogotá, Carlos Valencia Editores, 1978.

ROJAS DE PERDOMO, L. *Manual de arqueología colombiana*. Bogotá, Carlos Valencia Editores, 1986.

RUIZ GOMEZ, D. "El camión escalera." *Lámpara*, Vol. XXIV, no. 100: 23–29.

RUIZ ULLOA, J. "Sombrero suaza de jipi-japa o iraca." *Nueva revista colombiana de folklore*. Vol. 2, no. 8: 81–90.

SERPA ESPINOSA, R. "Cerámica." *La Revista de la academia de historia de Córdoba*. no. I, 1986: 13–15.

SERRANO, M. *Historia de la artesanía en Santander*. Bucaramanga, Artesanías de Colombia, 1988.

URICOECHEA, E. *El Dorado*. Berlin, F. Schneider and Co., 1854.

VASCO URIBE, L. G. *Semejantes a los dioses. Cerámica y cestería Emberá-Chamí*. Bogotá, Universidad Nacional de Colombia, 1987.

VILLA, E. "Consideraciones generales acerca del objeto artesanal." *Universitas Humanistica*. Vol. XII, no. 19: 19–37.

ZAMOSC, L. *El fique y los empaques en Colombia*. Bogotá, Editorial Dintel, 1981.

ZAPATA OLIVELLA, M. "Tres fuentes de la artesanía colombiana." *Revista colombiana de folklore*. Vol. III. no. 8: 2a: 147–150.

INDEX